• Dog Breed Handbooks •

Cocker Spaniel

• DOG BREED HANDBOOKS •

COCKER SPANIEL

DR. BRUCE FOGLE

SPECIAL PHOTOGRAPHY BY
TRACY MORGAN

DORLING KINDERSLEY
LONDON · NEW YORK · SYDNEY · MOSCOW

A DORLING KINDERSLEY BOOK
www.dk.com

Project Editor PHIL HUNT
Art Editor WENDY BARTLET
Editor SARAH LILLICRAPP
Designer HELEN THOMPSON
Managing Editor FRANCIS RITTER
Managing Art Editor DEREK COOMBES
DTP Designer CRESSIDA JOYCE
Production Controller RUTH CHARLTON

First published in Great Britain in 1996
by Dorling Kindersley Limited,
9 Henrietta Street, London WC2E 8PS

2 4 6 8 10 9 7 5 3

Copyright © 1996 Dorling Kindersley Limited,
London

Text copyright © 1996 Bruce Fogle

The right of Bruce Fogle to be identified
as Writer of this Work has been asserted by
him in accordance with the Copyright,
Designs, and Patents Act 1988.

All rights reserved. No part of this publication
may be reproduced, stored in a retrieval system,
or transmitted in any form or by any means,
electronic, mechanical, photocopying, recording
or otherwise without the prior permission
of the copyright owner.

A CIP catalogue record for this book is
available from the British Library

ISBN 0 7513 0339 9

Reproduced by Colourscan, Singapore
Printed in Hong Kong by Wing King Tong

CONTENTS

INTRODUCTION

To TRACE THE ORIGINS of today's domestic dog breeds one must go back over 12,000 years, to an era when only the dog's wolf ancestors existed. As semi-permanent human settlements began to spring up, wolves were attracted to this new environment because it was a source for scavenging and offered protection from predators. Natural food was scarce, however, and to survive in this habitat they became smaller and tamer.

It seems difficult to believe that the wolf is a relative, albeit distant, of the lovable Cocker Spaniel

In turn, the early human settlers realized that these animals could be used to their advantage, for hunting and protecting their camp sites. To this end, "wolf-dog" puppies were captured and raised within the communities.

THE CREATION OF BREEDS

From this pool of semi-domesticated dogs, various breeds evolved, with different attributes, so by 6,000 years ago, hunters and comforters existed as distinct canine groups. Small companion dogs were present in Europe at least 1,000 years ago, as were hunting dogs that followed scent trails,

As this early 16th-century calendar illustrates, small spaniels were used by falconers to scent game

pointed, or flushed game. These dogs accompanied the falconer, who captured game with nets. With the arrival of the gun, dogs were selectively bred not only to flush game, but also to retrieve it. The larger of these "Spaniels" worked on open ground, while smaller "Spaniels" worked in undergrowth. By selectively breeding for dogs with compact bodies, dense coats, and soft mouths, sportsmen created the Cocker Spaniel.

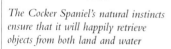

The Cocker Spaniel's natural instincts ensure that it will happily retrieve objects from both land and water

A Cocker Spaniel is the perfect addition to a family home, providing love and companionship

A HOME-LOVING HUNTER

The Cocker Spaniel and its American relative share a lovable nature and easy-going disposition that make them ideal companions in the home. Their willingness to please and considerable obedience skills have also led to substantial success at the highest levels in the show ring, but that does not mean that their hunting and retrieving characteristics have been abandoned. You only have to watch an energetic Cocker at play in the countryside to recognize its working roots.

THE PERFECT COMPANION

"A merry breed" is how the Cocker Spaniel has been described for hundreds of years and this is now even etched into the hallowed pages of the breed standard. Bred initially for driving game from undergrowth, Cockers are still adept in field trials today, exhibiting an extremely high standard of work. Even American Cockers bred for the show ring have retained the sturdy physical features of their working ancestors under their lavish coats. But it is the Cocker's loyalty and friendship that really stand out, and it is debatable whether there is a finer all-round companion in the canine world.

The American Cocker has the same affable personality as the Cocker Spaniel

The elegant Cocker Spaniel can be found in a wider range of colours than most other breeds, from jet black to the lightest cream

THE IDEAL CHOICE

THE COCKER SPANIEL'S excellent reputation as a family companion is justly deserved, but that does not mean that there is no work involved in keeping one. The thick, dense coat, especially the American's, needs daily attention, and frequent exercise is vital. Make sure your personality blends in with the Cocker's.

MOISTURE AND MUD

You may be attracted to the Cocker's dense, shiny, luxurious coat, but your dog's main ambition outdoors will be to attract vegetation, moisture, and mud. The long feathers on the legs, belly, and ears are prone to burrs and other adhesive objects. You should check your Cocker's coat for unwanted matter after each exercise period.

PREPARE FOR HAIR!

A Cocker's coat may look permanent, but it is not; Cockers moult surprisingly large amounts of hair for their size. Daily grooming is necessary, with the ears demanding special attention after exercise and eating. If the coat becomes too matted, it may be necessary to cut it all off. American Cockers with show-quality coats need particular attention because of the density of their hair.

BOUNDING WITH ENERGY

All Cockers, but especially Americans, have unlimited energy. Even though they are small dogs, Cockers will attempt to lick visitors' faces, and this can be annoying. Choose a Cocker Spaniel only if you are willing to provide your dog with a safe outlet for its energy demands, and are prepared for occasional accidental mayhem at home. This is even more likely if your lively, inquisitive Cocker is left home alone for any length of time.

An excitable Cocker will jump up onto your legs if given the chance

THE NEED TO CARRY — A RESPONSIBLE OUTDOOR WORKER

When a Cocker picks up its lead and brings it to you it is amusing. But when it presents your used socks to visitors it can be more exasperating. Accept the fact that your Cocker will feel the need to carry items in its mouth and that embarrassing situations might occur as a result!

Most Cocker Spaniels are kept as companions, but they were bred to work and thrive on frequent, robust mental and physical activity. Although Cockers will spend much of their lives indoors, they are not lap dogs content to live centrally-heated, cosseted lives – they need vigorous daily exercise. You should make time in your schedule to accommodate this if you are considering acquiring one.

CARED FOR AS ONE OF THE FAMILY

The responsible, easy-to-train, affectionate Cocker Spaniel will only make an ideal family companion if you are willing to utilize its superb evolutionary development by providing sensible and considerate training. Good family dogs do not appear spontaneously; they are good companions because their training has been good. You must make a commitment to invest time and energy in your Cocker's proper development.

Dog enriches family life, but is reliant on you

THE COCKER SPANIEL

THE NEATLY PACKAGED, moderately sized Cocker Spaniel was originally developed by breeders who wanted a small gundog suitable for use in dense undergrowth. As the breed's popularity as a companion increased, standards evolved emphasizing temperament and coat texture. Today's Cocker is a lovable creature especially suited to the family home.

COMPACT AND MUSCULAR
The Cocker's compact body is surprisingly well muscled under its dense protective coat and is set on well-boned, sturdy legs. A double coat of hair protects the forelegs and the thick pads on the feet are protected by dense hair between the toes.

SKULL
Softly contoured skull has no sharp angles, a distinct, moderately grooved stop, and strong jaws capable of carrying game

BACK
Neck blends with back in a gentle curve; back slopes slightly towards gently rounded rump

NECK
Graceful and muscular, arches slightly at the skull

SHOULDERS
Sloping shoulders with flat blades; same length as upper arms

FORELEGS
Robust, straight legs almost uniform in size from elbow to heel

FEET
Firm, round, "cat-like" feet have excellent webbing between the toes; hair needs routine clipping

GENTLE-LOOKING AND DIGNIFIED

There is no coarseness to a Cocker Spaniel; its expression is invariably soft and accommodating. Even when actively alert, its low-set ears and warm eyes make it heart-meltingly attractive.

EYES
Set wide apart, medium-sized, dark brown, and slightly oval; well-fitting lids

EARS
Set low at nose level and close to the skull; long feathering frames the face and enhances soft expression

OFFICIAL BREED STANDARDS

A breed standard is simply a "blueprint" which acts as a guideline for breeders. Although breed standards are precise, interpretation varies according to individual breeders and judges. As fashions change, the interpretation of the breed standard also changes. If trends swing sufficiently in a particular direction, a breed standard is rewritten, incorporating new standards. This has happened several times with the Cocker Spaniel. For example, the need for a docked tail has been dropped in some countries where this is seen as a needless mutilation, but is retained in others.

BODY
Compact body is solid without appearing heavy and deep chest with brisket reaches to elbows; bottom of chest slopes to moderate tuck-up at waist

A STURDY, WELL-PROPORTIONED BODY

The Cocker's desire to retrieve, combined with its compact, insulated body, makes it ideal for working in dense undergrowth. Its willingness to respond to command also suits working to the gun or obedience training. Its luxurious coat, gentle expression, and convenient size make it equally attractive as a popular companion.

TAIL
Carried horizontally but always rapid in action; higher and even more active when excited

HINDQUARTERS
Well-rounded and relatively broad hips with plenty of propulsive muscle power

DOUBLE COAT
Dense, waterproof, shiny coat is soft to touch and shortest over the back

---

MEASUREMENTS (BRITISH BREED STANDARD)
Height at withers (see page 75):
FEMALE 38–39 cm (15–15½ in)
MALE 39–41 cm (15½–16 in)
Weight, in proportion to height:
FEMALE 12–14.5 kg (26–32 lb)
MALE 13–15.5 kg (28–34 lb)

1.8 m (6 ft)

THE AMERICAN COCKER

THE SMALLEST OF ALL GUNDOGS, the American Cocker was created in a relatively short period of time from the breeding of selected Cocker Spaniels. It has a more pronounced stop between the skull, a shorter muzzle, more domed head, and a more luxurious coat than its English cousin, but possesses an equally loyal, affectionate temperament.

COAT
Short, fine, silky hair on head; well-feathered ears, chest, abdomen, and legs cover protective undercoat

A ROUNDER SKULL
The American Cocker has a slightly domed, rounded skull, with a "well-chiselled" bone structure beneath its eyes that readily differentiates it from the Cocker Spaniel. Beneath the dense coat is a firmly muscled, solidly boned body.

BACK
Strong, straight back slopes evenly downwards from the shoulders to the base of the tail

TAIL
Carried in a line with the body; slightly higher when alert

FEET
Compact and rounded, with thick pads, good webbing, and close-knit hair

THE VALUE OF BREED STANDARDS

Breed standards provide an excellent guideline for breeders to follow, but when characteristics are taken to the extreme, the results can be detrimental to a breed. Some people, for example, feel that the "show quality" American Cocker's intensely thick coat, heavy-all-over feathering, and shorter, deeper muzzle have led unwittingly to increases in skin problems and the incidence of epilepsy. Recent breed standards have deliberately avoided words that might promote exaggerated characteristics.

AFFABLE, INNOCENT FACE
Selective breeding has given the American Cocker a high dome, accentuated stop, and short, deep muzzle. Breeders actually selected these "infant-like" features when the American Cocker was being developed.

LIPS
Full upper lip covers lower jaw, but is not excessively pendulous

SKULL
No tendency to flatness; rounded but not exaggerated, with pronounced eyebrows and a distinct stop

NECK
Slightly arched, with no drooping "throatiness"; rises strongly from shoulders

EYES
Alert and appealing dark, round eyes with well-fitted eyelids

SHOULDERS
Clean-cut, do not protrude, and slope back gently

NOSE
Typical large nostrils of a game-seeking dog; same colour as the eye rims

EARS
Long and lobular ears, on a line with the eyes, have thin skin under dense hair

ROBUST, BALANCED, AND REFINED
In spite of its profuse coat of hair and relatively small, compact body, the American Cocker Spaniel is a gundog and therefore capable of endurance and surprising speed. It has a well-balanced physique, and is able to perform in the field or in the rigours of advanced obedience training.

MEASUREMENTS (BRITISH BREED STANDARD)
Height at withers (see page 77):
FEMALE 33.75–36.25 cm (13½–14½ in)
MALE 36.25–38.75 cm (14½–15½ in)
Weight, in proportion to height:
FEMALE 11–12 kg (24–26 lb)
MALE 12–13 kg (26–28 lb)

1.8 m (6 ft)

BEHAVIOUR PROFILES

ENGLISH AND AMERICAN Cocker Spaniels are quite similar in their manners. Both, for example, are remarkably tolerant of other dogs. However, selective breeding has produced pronounced differences in their behaviour, which is also influenced by environmental factors.

TRAINABILITY/OBEDIENCE

With working backgrounds, both breeds are more trainable than average dogs. Cockers are generally more responsive to obedience training than their American cousins.

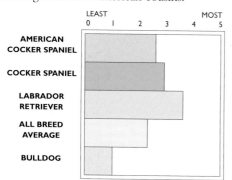

PLAYFULNESS WITH OTHER DOGS

Cocker Spaniels are more playful than average with other dogs, which is not too surprising if you consider their gregarious, inquisitive personalities and need for exercise.

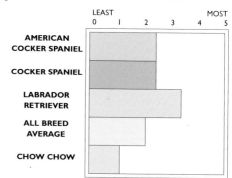

BARKING TO PROTECT THE HOME

Cockers may be small, but they often bark at strangers entering their territory. Although less dominant than other breeds, they exhibit higher levels of protective aggression.

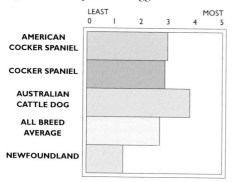

EXCITABILITY

Cockers have high energy levels and are more excitable than the average dog – similar to the yellow Labrador. They are demonstrative, but their excitement sometimes leads to whining.

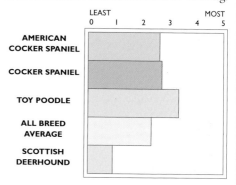

How to Use the Behaviour Charts

In a recent study, vets and dog breeders have assessed over 100 breeds, rating each on a scale of 0–5 for specific personality traits, with 0 representing the lowest score among all dogs and 5 the highest. By comparing Cocker Spaniels and American Cocker Spaniels to the average for all breeds, and to the highest and lowest recorded scores, it is possible to make cross-breed comparisons. These findings do not take sex or coat colour into consideration.

Reliable with Strange Children

Surprisingly for such family dogs, Cockers, especially Americans, are more likely than average to regard strange children with suspicion. This is more common in females.

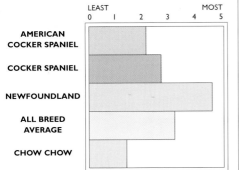

Calm in New Circumstances

Although bred to work to the gun, years of breeding for leisure rather than for work have diminished the Cocker's need for calm when presented with unexpected sounds.

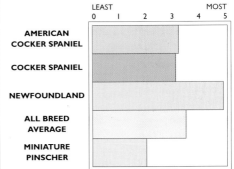

Destructive when Alone

Cockers are less likely than average to be destructive when left alone. Scratching, digging in carpets, or chewing furniture is less common in well-exercised dogs.

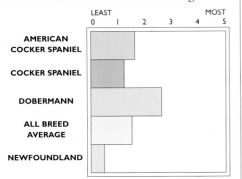

House Trainable

Most dogs respond well to house training; the American is about average, the Cocker is easier to house train. This is influenced more by early training than by breeding.

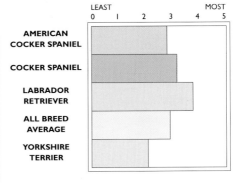

COATS AND COLOURS

COCKER SPANIELS HAVE a richer variety of colours than perhaps any other breed. Genetically, black is dominant to all other colours. Other solid colours are genetically dominant to mixed colours, which is why vivacious tricolours like black, white, and tan or blue roan and tan are relatively uncommon.

WIDE-RANGING COLOURATIONS

Cocker coats are classified into solids and parti-colours. Included in solids are black, chocolate, deep autumn red, liver, and light cream; black or brown and tan also comes under this grouping, with tan points on specific areas of the body, such as in spots over the eyes. Parti-colours are coats of two or more distinct colours, one of which is white; these are subdivided into ticked, roaned, mixed, and tricolours. A ticked coat is primarily white with one or two colours through its hair; a roan has more colour than a ticked, with white more evenly blended; a mixed dog has two well-broken colours, one of which is white; and tricolours have three solid blocks of colour. Breeders rarely cross solids with parti-colours.

BLUE ROAN
This is a popular mix of black and white. Roans also occur in orange, lemon, and liver.

SOLID COLOURS
Black dominates all solids – if one parent is black, there is a 50 per cent chance of each puppy in the litter being black. Chocolate was developed as a solid colour fairly recently.

ORANGE-AND-WHITE
Mixed colours actually predate solid colours, and existed in spaniels well before Cockers were recognised as a distinct breed.

COAT LENGTH AND TEXTURE

American Cockers usually have longer coats than their English cousins because they are bred primarily as show dogs rather than working dogs. In terms of texture, the darker the colour the denser the coat. Light coloured coats are silkier than the darker colours; parti-coloured and tan dogs will have a mixture of dense and fine hair. Ticked coats are also silky and have less feathering than dark coats. Some breeders feel that chocolate coats have a tendency to be woolly.

PUPPY PAW COLOURS

It is sometimes possible to tell the adult colour of puppies born with light coats by looking at the colour of their pads. For example, newborn puppies with black pads and noses are likely to become blue roans as adults. Puppies born with pink or pink and black flecked pads and noses may develop black and white coats or even black and white ticked coats later in life.

BROWN-AND-TAN
For showing purposes, tan should be 10 per cent or less of the colour.

BUFF COAT
This is a recent colour in terms of Cocker evolution, with a wide range of shades to choose from.

TRICOLOURED
This is genetically one of the most complicated coat patterns.

BLACK-AND-WHITE
The striking contrast between black and white in this American Cocker's luxuriant coat makes it a popular parti-colour for breeders.

PIGMENT AND PERSONALITY

SCIENTISTS HAVE KNOWN for some time that there is a link between coat colour and temperament. This link is probably the colour pigment melanin, which is biochemically similar to chemicals that act as transmitters in the brain. Cocker Spaniel behaviour has been studied in more detail than any other breed.

RESULTS OF THE SURVEYS

A MOST AMENABLE BREED

According to a study made by Cambridge University, England, Cocker Spaniels are more playful and trainable, and less aggressive than most dogs. However, in some circumstances, individual Cockers may guard their food or even challenge children, although this is no more of a problem than it is with other breeds. The willingness of the British Cocker Spaniel Club to participate in this research means that this type of behaviour is better understood in Cocker Spaniels than it is in other types of dog.

A red Cocker's temperament can be controlled through early basic training

FIERY RED HEADS

The Cambridge study – involving over 1,000 Cocker Spaniel households throughout Britain – concluded that solid colour Cockers were more likely to be aggressive in 12 out of 13 situations. Red/golden Cockers were shown to be the most aggressive of all, in situations involving strangers, family members, while being disciplined, and sometimes for no apparent reason.

OTHER COLOUR-RELATED DIFFERENCES

In a separate vets' study of 100 breeds of dog, questions were also asked about a variety of behaviours within the Cocker and American Cocker Spaniel breeds according to coat colour. The results show that there are well-defined differences in Cocker behaviour other than those that appeared in the Cambridge studies. The lowest possible score on the charts is 0, the highest 5. These results apply to the whole breed, not individual dogs.

PLAYFULNESS WITH OTHER DOGS

While black Cockers are typical of their breed, reds are a little less likely to play with other strange dogs. Parti-colours, here as black and whites, are a little more likely to instigate or respond to play. Blacks and reds also demand more physical activity than parti-colours.

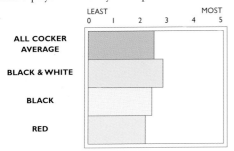

RELIABLE WITH STRANGE CHILDREN

Black Cockers are slightly better than average when confronted by a five-year-old child on their own territory; reds are less reliable than average. Black and whites come out on top, and they, along with blacks, are more willing than reds to accept strangers in their homes.

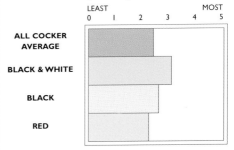

DESTRUCTIVE WHEN LEFT ALONE

Black Cockers are breed average in their likelihood to chew carpets or scratch wallpaper when left at home alone; reds are slightly more likely to be destructive, and black and whites are the least destructive. They are also less excitable than blacks and reds.

DISOBEDIENT TOWARDS OWNERS

Once again it is black Cockers who are average in their likelihood to disobey owners, while reds are more likely to do so and black and whites less likely. Early training is just as important as genetic factors and will smooth out most of these cross-colour differences.

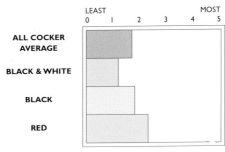

SEX AND TYPE DIFFERENCES

COCKER SPANIELS AND AMERICAN COCKERS show fewer sex-related differences in behaviour than many other breeds; size differences are correspondingly small. The greatest variations between individuals bred for work and those destined for the show ring or family companionship are in how they are trained.

PHYSIQUE AND TEMPERAMENT: THE SEXES COMPARED

Male Cockers are only marginally larger than females and share their gentle looks. There are virtually no differences between the sexes in ease of house training, nervousness, destructiveness, whining for attention, excitability, or need for activity.

GENTLE, RESPONSIVE FEMALE
Female Cockers are considered easier to obedience train, but there is no difference in the trainability of female and male Americans. Females of both breeds are less likely to be disobedient to their owners than males. Female Cockers, however, demand more petting than males and are more likely to bark anxiously. They will also be more aggressive to other household dogs.

GENTLE, ASSURED MALE
Males tend to be slightly more assertive, with male Cockers more likely to bark protectively in their homes. Both males, especially the Cocker, are more wary of strangers. American Cocker males can sometimes be a little unreliable with unknown children. Males are more likely to be aggressive towards strange dogs.

GENDER-SPECIFIC MEDICAL PROBLEMS

A variety of diseases are caused or influenced by sex hormones. Unless spayed early in life, females of all breeds may suffer from breast cancer and pyometra, or womb infection. Spaying will eliminate the risk of these problems. Males sometimes get tumours around the anus, testicular cancer, or prostate inflammation or cancer, with associated pain or bleeding when attempting to urinate. Again, neutering is the best treatment, but the Cocker's tendency to gain weight means that diet must be controlled after neutering.

SHOW OR WORKING TYPE?

BRED FOR BEAUTY

Virtually all American Cockers and most Cockers are bred to show standards. While the American's breed standard states that its coat should not hide the dog's true shape, in practice the most densely-coated dogs often win shows. Breeders of Cocker Spaniels have adhered more to their standard, which states that feathering should not interfere with field work.

American Cockers will continue to be bred virtually exclusively for the show ring

Long coat is a characteristic of the American Cocker

TRAINED TO WORK

Although the Cocker Spaniel is still bred as a working dog, working Cockers look very similar to their show-ring relatives. They are often slimmer because their physical exercise enhances body tone. Almost all American Cockers are show dogs, but a small number do participate in agility and obedience trials.

NEUTERING AND AGGRESSION

Some dogs are neutered for social reasons, others for behavioural problems. Neutering reduces the intensity of aggression between males, but this is not really a problem with Cocker Spaniels. Neutering is unlikely to reduce a Cocker's aggression towards other family members. Spaying has little effect on females except in naturally dominant bitches; they may become more aggressive.

THE RIGHT START

IF YOU HAVE NOT YET DECIDED which type of Cocker Spaniel you
want, get further advice from experts and then choose carefully
according to your desires and lifestyle. Have your home
prepared for the arrival of your new puppy, and begin your
novice companion's life with you as you mean to continue.

ADVICE ON WHERE TO BUY

VETERINARY CLINIC
Your local veterinary clinic is an excellent
source of unbiased, informed advice on
what to look for in a healthy puppy. Dog
training clubs will also often be able to
recommend specific breeders who can
provide puppies and sometimes adults too.

ANIMAL RESCUE CENTRES
Dog shelters and rescue centres often have
adult Cockers in need of new homes. These
dogs may take some time to settle in to
their new home, but can eventually make
devoted companions. As with all "recycled"
individuals, however, they may well harbour
unexpected personality quirks.

DECIDING ON A PUPPY OR A DOG

Puppies are both appealing and exasperating.
Acquiring a puppy means that you can mould
its behaviour to fit your family's lifestyle. When
viewing a litter, watch how the puppies behave,
decide which sex you prefer, and select a
puppy that seems bright, alert, and healthy.
Be prepared to invest
time and energy in
initial house and
obedience training.
If this is too
daunting, consider
getting a trained
adult Cocker.

Healthy puppy
feels firm, and is
surprisingly heavy

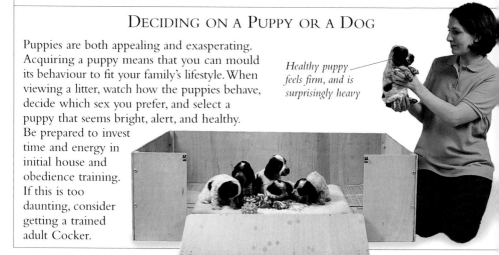

Settling in at Home

Secure crate allows gentle exposure to new environment

Getting Acquainted

Your new puppy is likely to feel disoriented when it first arrives in your home. Initially restrict it to just one room in the house. Offer it food, water, and a chewable toy, preferably in a crate. Provide soft bedding in one section for it to lie on and have an equal area of newspaper for toileting. If you have another pet, keep it in a separate room until your puppy is asleep.

First Night Alone

The first night that your puppy is away from its mother and litter is the hardest. The crate will provide a safe "den", and with a little perseverance your puppy will settle down and sleep in it. Initially keep the crate in your bedroom and get up once each night for the first few weeks to take your puppy to relieve itself.

Health Checks for Your New Dog

Arrange for your vet to examine your new Cocker, and make any purchase conditional on your vet's confirmation that the dog is healthy. It will be examined for signs of parasites, infection, malnutrition, and congenital or inherited diseases. The law states that if a puppy is not healthy at the time of sale, you are entitled to a refund or replacement.

Meet the Parents

Responsible breeders, both amateur and professional, are proud of their stock and will be delighted to introduce you to the litter's mother and also the father if available. The parents' appearance and behaviour will give you an idea of your puppy's mature size and likely temperament. Be cautious with individuals who are unable to show you the puppy's mother; they may not be genuine breeders but acting as agents for puppy farms where Cockers are bred purely for profit – often in uncaring, unhygienic conditions.

EARLY TRAINING

COCKERS ARE EXCELLENT LEARNERS. They respond willingly when rewarded with praise, petting, food treats, and toys. Start gentle obedience and house training as soon as your puppy arrives in its new home, and maintain contact with other dogs to ensure proper social development.

LEARNING WITH REWARDS

VERBAL PRAISE

Cocker Spaniels are enthusiastic pupils; be just as enthusiastic when giving commands to your puppy. Even youthful eight-week-old puppies understand when you are genuinely pleased with their behaviour. Positive words of praise should always accompany any food and touch rewards.

Puppy knows it has done well when it hears "Good dog!"

STROKING REWARD

A stroke from you is a potent reward for your puppy. Your Cocker will naturally want to be stroked, but do not comply on demand. Instead, give a gentle command, then reward obedience with petting.

ACQUIRING SOCIAL SKILLS

A puppy's ability to learn is at its greatest during the first three months. If denied ongoing contact with other dogs during this important stage, your Cocker Spaniel may not develop the social skills necessary for meeting strange dogs later in life. If you do not have another dog, ask your vet to help you organize regular supervised "puppy parties" to encourage natural, friendly interaction between puppies of a similar age. If you take your puppy out for a walk, be on the lookout for potentially aggressive dogs; confrontation could be a traumatic experience for the puppy.

Favourite foods are useful as rewards for good behaviour

FOOD TREAT

Most Cockers respond well to food rewards but some may be indifferent. Experiment with various food snacks to discover what your puppy likes most, then use this treat as a food reward, combining it with verbal praise.

TOYS FOR YOUR NEW PUPPY

SUITABLE TOYS FOR CHEWING AND PLAYING

As natural hunters, Cocker Spaniels enjoy playing with toys, especially squeaky ones. Keep a maximum of four toys for your Cocker, ones it can chase, retrieve, capture, and chew. Some Cockers can be possessive about their toys, so make sure your dog sees you put the toys away – it will then understand that they belong to you.

TOYS AS REWARD AND COMFORT

While toys left lying around soon become boring, items brought out only under special circumstances are transformed into exciting rewards. When given selectively as a prize for good behaviour, toys can serve as extremely effective training aids. Whenever you leave your Cocker alone, at any age, provide it with a well-loved toy as a comforting distraction.

HOUSE TRAINING INDOORS AND OUT

PAPER TRAINING

Your puppy will usually want to eliminate after waking, eating, drinking, or exercise. It may signal this by putting its nose down and sniffing. Quickly place the dog in an area covered with newspaper, and praise it when it urinates or messes. It is pointless to punish your puppy after an accident. If you catch it in the act, however, sternly say "No" to teach it that it must use the paper.

MOVING OUTSIDE

Start outdoor training as soon as possible. Three-month-old puppies need to empty their bladders about every four hours. Take a small piece of soiled paper with you; the puppy will smell its own scent, and be encouraged to transfer toileting outside. As it eliminates, say "Hurry up"; this will train your dog to relieve itself on that command.

INTRODUCING OUTDOORS

PUPPIES SHOULD EXPERIENCE the outdoors as soon as possible. If you have access to a garden, introduce your Cocker Spaniel to its collar and lead and supply suitable identification. Do not wait for chance meetings with people – create situations where your new puppy learns about life under controlled circumstances.

IDENTIFICATION

STANDARD NAME TAG
Engraved or canister tags carry vital information about your dog, including a contact telephone number and your vet's telephone number for emergencies. Metal canisters have a tendency to unscrew; apply a dab of nail varnish to prevent this happening.

Registration number is stored in this tiny microchip

PERMANENT METHODS
A tiny microchip, encased in glass, permanently stores important data. Inserted just under the skin on the neck, it provides safe and secure information that can be "read" using a hand-held scanner. Painless tattoos are another permanent alternative that might be available in your area.

INTRODUCTION TO COLLAR AND LEAD

1 Collar and lead training can begin as soon as you acquire your puppy. Start by letting your Cocker see and smell the collar. Then, avoiding eye contact, kneel down and put the collar on the puppy, distracting it with words. Reward it with treats, physical contact, and praise. Actively play for a while, then take the collar off. Your puppy will quickly learn to associate the collar with rewards, and should accept it without reluctance.

Owner talks to puppy while collar is attached and puppy remains calm

2 Once your puppy is content wearing its collar, kneel in front and attach a lead. Keeping the lead slack, entice your dog to one side with a toy or food reward. When it moves towards the reward, apply light tension to the lead. Allow the puppy to have the toy or treat, and give it praise.

MEETING STRANGERS

Arrange for a friend to meet you and your dog outdoors. Ask your friend to kneel down to greet the puppy, because this will help dissuade it from jumping up. Also discourage direct eye contact – this reduces the chance of an overly submissive response such as rolling over, common in some young Cockers. Finally, give your friend a food treat to give to your puppy.

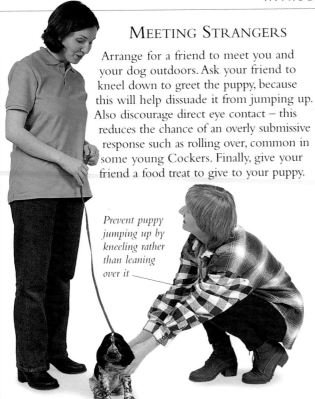

Prevent puppy jumping up by kneeling rather than leaning over it

ESSENTIAL PUPPY INOCULATIONS

Your vet will vaccinate your new puppy against a range of infectious diseases such as distemper, hepatitis, and canine parvovirus. For extra protection, your vet may advise that your puppy avoids contact with unfamiliar dogs for a few weeks. Social contact with known healthy dogs should continue, however, and is vital for proper social development.

ENCOUNTERING OTHER DOGS

Ask a friend with a placid dog to meet you while you are walking your puppy. Have your friend instruct her dog to remain calm while you walk past, and reward your puppy's own calm response with treats and praise.

If you have no friends with dogs, you will find that other dog walkers are more than willing to help with this form of training. Through routine meetings, your puppy learns that there is no need to be fearful of other dogs. Regular interaction with puppies of a similar age will also help in developing vital social skills.

Well-behaved adult dog does not provoke puppy

Puppy shows interest in strange dog but no anxiety

FIRST ROUTINES

A PUPPY'S EARLY EXPERIENCES mould its life-long personality, so you should start as you mean to continue. Train your Cocker to be left alone, to come to you on command, and most importantly, to understand that you and your family are its superiors and will not put up with any misbehaviour.

ACCEPTING BEING LEFT ALONE

Owner walks away, giving hand signal that puppy will soon learn means "Wait"

No matter how much you enjoy being with your new puppy, there will be times when you must leave it on its own. Train your young Cocker to accept that this is part of its routine by confining it to its crate with an interesting reward, such as a hollow toy filled with a little peanut butter. Then quietly walk away, signalling "Wait". Gradually accustom your dog to being left alone for extended periods.

Puppy is content in crate because it has been rewarded with favourite toy

ASSERT YOUR LEADERSHIP

Some Cocker Spaniels have a tendency to be pushy with their owners, to resist being groomed or handled, and even to snap at members of the household. Start grooming routines with your puppy from an early age and teach it the meaning of a stern "No!". A painless physical reprimand, such as mimicking its mother by grabbing the scruff of the neck, should be used only for theatrical effect and very sparingly.

SEVERAL PUPPIES?

If you have more than one puppy, train them individually for effective results. It is very difficult, even for highly experienced dog handlers, to maintain the concentration of several lively puppies together!

COMING TO YOU ON COMMAND

1 For safety and responsible control, your puppy must learn always to come to you on command. Use positive training with rewards; never call your puppy to discipline it, or it will then associate returning to you with being reprimanded. Having trained your Cocker to accept a collar and lead, put these on the dog and kneel a short distance away, with the lead tucked securely under one knee. Hold a chewable or attractively scented toy as a reward; this will be more clearly visible than a food treat.

Appealing toy makes training fun for your dog

2 Call your puppy's name in a clear, friendly tone to attract its attention. When it turns its head towards you, give the command "Come" and wave the toy as an enticement. Keep the lead slack; do not reel in your puppy but encourage it to come willingly.

Call your puppy by name with a welcoming tone of voice

3 Greet your puppy with open arms. Out of curiosity, it should walk towards you. As it moves, say "Good dog" in an enthusiastic voice. When the puppy reaches you, reward it with the toy. Never call your dog to discipline it – train it to understand that the command "Come" is a positive one.

Puppy responds and walks towards the toy

COME, SIT, DOWN, STAY

TRAINING YOUR PUPPY to come, sit, lie down, and stay down is most important for the safety of your dog and for harmonious relations with your family, friends, and in situations outside the home. As a breed, the Cocker Spaniel is a delight to work with and exceptionally responsive to basic obedience training.

COME AND SIT

Maintain eye contact with your puppy

1 Try to work in a quiet, narrow space such as a hallway, without any distractions. Holding the puppy on a loose lead, cheerfully call its name and let it see that you have a food treat in your hand. As it begins to move, give the command "Come". Be enthusiastic, and while your puppy walks towards you, praise it by saying "Good dog".

The lead permits gentle reinforcement of the command

2 When your puppy reaches you, move the treat above its head. To keep its eye on the food, the puppy will naturally sit. As it does so, issue the command "Sit" and immediately give the reward. Repeat the exercise regularly until your puppy responds to words alone.

Offer reward calmly to avoid overexcitement

The puppy turns its head towards the trainer and naturally sits

THE VALUE OF "NO!"

"No!" is one of the first, and most important, words your Cocker should learn. When your puppy understands its meaning, you are in control and accidents are prevented. Just as you use a friendly voice and warm, appealing body language to make training fun for your puppy, adopt a stern tone when issuing this reprimand. There is no need to shout or even raise your voice. Teach the meaning of the "No" command during general training, but no matter how frustrated you are, never use it to finish a training session. Always finish on a positive note.

Puppy stretches along floor to receive food treat

FOLLOW DOWN

1 Kneel beside the seated puppy, holding its collar with one hand, and place a treat by its nose. If your puppy will not sit or tries to get up, tuck its hindquarters under with your free hand and command "Sit".

2 Move the treat forwards and down in an arc, drawing the puppy as it follows the food with its nose. As it starts to lie down, give the command "Down". If the puppy refuses, gently raise its front legs into a begging position, then lower it down, always rewarding obedience with gentle praise.

The puppy remains in the sit position because it is comfortable

3 Still holding the collar, continue to move the treat forwards and down until your puppy is lying completely flat. Then reward the puppy with the treat and praise. Do not praise excessively, however, as this can excite your young Cocker and be counter-productive.

STAY DOWN

For its own safety, your Cocker should learn to "stay down" until you give the command to move. With the lead still attached, kneel beside the puppy and press gently on its shoulders. After a few seconds, release your puppy, saying "Okay". Do not use food rewards here as they are too exciting. Only train for short periods when you and your puppy are mentally alert.

Gradually extend length of "Stay" to minutes

WALKING TO HEEL

EXUBERANT COCKER SPANIELS love investigating the outdoors.
Ensure that walking your Cocker is a pleasure rather than a
struggle by training it from a young age to walk to heel.
Start by training your puppy indoors without a lead, then
graduate to lead training both inside and outside your home.

WALKING TO HEEL WITHOUT A LEAD

1 In a quiet indoor location, kneel to the right of your alert, seated puppy. Holding its collar with your left hand, speak its name and show it a food treat in your other hand.

2 Using the scent of the food to attract the puppy, get up and walk in a straight line while giving the command "Heel". Be ready to grasp the collar with your left hand and return it to the correct heel position if the puppy wanders. When you stop, command "Wait".

Puppy eagerly follows reward

3 Keeping the treat low to prevent your puppy from jumping up, bend your knees and turn right, drawing the food around as you move. Repeat the command "Heel". Your puppy will speed up to walk around you.

Train puppy to stay close to your leg

4 Left turns are more difficult. Hold the collar with your left hand and give the command "Steady". Place the reward close to your dog's mouth, then move it to the left. The puppy will follow.

Puppy turns to left in pursuit of reward

Heelwork with a Lead

1 With the puppy on a long training lead and seated to your left, hold the lead and a treat in your right hand, and the slack of the lead in your left. Tell your puppy to sit.

Puppy watches owner intently

Maintain eye contact as puppy waits for next command

2 Move forwards on your left foot and give the command "Heel". If your puppy pulls, command it to sit. Do not shout or lose concentration.

3 With the puppy beside you in the heel position, offer it the reward and say "Good dog". Repeat the "Sit. Heel. Wait." sequence.

5 Once the right turn has been learned, begin left-turn training. Hold the treat in front of the puppy's nose to slow it down while speeding up your own circling movement to the left. Keep the puppy close to your left leg and issue the command "Steady" as it follows you around.

4 After the dog has learned to walk to heel in a straight line, teach it to turn to the right by guiding it with the treat. Do not pull or get angry; build up confidence with praise.

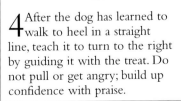

Puppy slows down while concentrating on food reward

INDOOR TRAINING

ALTHOUGH COCKER SPANIELS were bred for an outdoor life, your dog is likely to spend most of its time in your home. Ensure it understands that you make and enforce the rules. Provide it with its own bed to retire to and give it satisfying time and attention, but on your own terms.

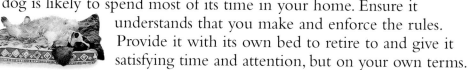

LEARNING TO WAIT PATIENTLY

They may be small, but Cockers are adept at subtly becoming leaders of the pack. Do not let your dog initiate activity and do not respond to its demands for attention. Your Spaniel will need its own private space, so by giving it a bed or crate it can regard as its own, it will retire there while you relax or get on with other household activities. Place the bed in a busy area of the house such as the kitchen; this way your sociable Cocker will not feel isolated.

Quilt-type bed is comfortable and large enough for adult dog to stretch out fully

SPENDING QUALITY TIME TOGETHER

Nurture the bond between you and your dog. Set time aside each day to offer your Cocker a little physical and mental activity. This time will strengthen your relationship, and reinforce basic obedience training. Vary the time and type of activity, otherwise your Cocker will learn to expect a certain game at a certain time. Put toys away at the end of play; this will make their next appearance more exciting.

Playing with your dog will keep it happy and alert, and is rewarding for both parties

MEETING STRANGERS IN THE HOME

Cocker Spaniels can be surprisingly territorial, so you should train your dog to sit when a visitor arrives. This will reduce the potential of territory guarding – more common in males and solid colours – and will also control the tendency for some Cockers to go wild with joyful excitement. To reinforce calm, ask your visitor to disregard your pet at first. Reward good behaviour with approving words, a stroke, and occasionally a food treat.

Dog sits attentively while visitor is greeted

RELINQUISHING A FORBIDDEN ITEM

Any Cocker Spaniel is likely to hoard items lying around the house, such as tea towels, socks, gloves, and slippers, and take them to its bed. Reduce the potential for this unwanted behaviour by training your dog, using food treats, to drop and surrender any item willingly on command.

UNDERSTANDING WHAT IS WRONG

Use body language as well as words to convey your displeasure

A dog will not know that it has done something wrong until it has been told. Lying on a comfortable chair, for instance, will seem perfectly natural to your Cocker. Use assertive body language and a stern voice to reprimand your dog when it does something that is not permitted. Perfect timing is essential in this task. If you discipline your dog some time after the event, it will understand that you are angry, but not why.

OUTSIDE THE HOME

FOR ITS OWN PROTECTION and the safety of others, you must keep your Cocker under secure control in your own garden or further afield. If planning a holiday, make sure that your dog will be safe and comfortable if left with others while you are away. Always observe social obligations conscientiously.

HOME AND AWAY

If you need to kennel your dog while you are away, visit recommended kennels and look for cleanliness and security. A good alternative is a dog-sitting service; your vet may be able to supply you with details.

BE CONSIDERATE TO OTHERS

Obey local dog control regulations and clean up when your dog messes. Carry a supply of plastic bags to use as "poop scoops" and deposit these in special waste bins if available. Do not let your dog be a nuisance to others.

CONTROL OUTDOORS

HEAD HALTER

A fitted head halter offers more control than a standard collar, especially for strong-willed Cockers. If your Cocker pulls on its lead, its own momentum will pull its head downward in an inhibiting manner.

HALF-CHECK COLLAR

This is the most common control for Cockers. Fit the collar so that the soft webbing lies round your dog's throat, with the chain at the back of its neck. A tug on the lead will tighten the collar.

MUZZLE

Apply a muzzle either to obey local laws or to prevent your dog from biting. Use a basket variety in the correct size and properly adjusted to permit panting and barking. Never leave your muzzled dog unattended for long periods.

Safe Travelling by Car

Train your dog from an early age to travel in the back of a car. Ensure your Cocker's safety, as well as your own, by securing it in the back seat with a special canine seat belt that, like a child's harness, attaches to the standard seat belt anchors. Alternatively, restrict your dog to the back of an estate car fitted with a sturdy, purpose-made dog grille.

Cars are Deathtraps

Heatstroke is one of the most common causes of preventable death in Cocker Spaniels; a dog cannot sweat other than through its pads. Its dense coat magnifies heat and in hot conditions its body temperature rises swiftly and critically. Cockers can die within minutes when there is no escape from a hot car. Never leave your dog in your car – even parked in the shade or with the window slightly opened – in warm or sunny weather. In cold weather, do not leave your dog in brilliant sunshine with the car engine running and the heater on high – it can be just as lethal.

Planning a Safe and Secure Garden

The greatest hazard presented by your garden is the risk of escape. Check that all fencing is sturdy, gate latches secure, and that hedges have no gaps. Install wire mesh where necessary. Keep all garden chemicals safely locked away, and if you have outdoor lighting, ensure that no cables are exposed and may be chewed. To prevent damage to your lawn, train your dog to use a specific site as its toilet. Store all waste and any horticultural tools securely out of reach, and do not establish plants that may be poisonous to dogs. Always watch your Cocker carefully near a lit barbecue to ensure that it does not lick hot implements, and cover garden ponds to prevent your dog paddling.

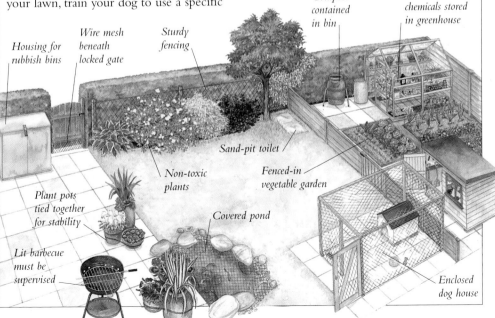

Housing for rubbish bins

Wire mesh beneath locked gate

Sturdy fencing

Compost contained in bin

Garden chemicals stored in greenhouse

Plant pots tied together for stability

Non-toxic plants

Sand-pit toilet

Fenced-in vegetable garden

Covered pond

Lit barbecue must be supervised

Enclosed dog house

CONSTRUCTIVE PLAY

COCKER SPANIELS MAY BE relatively small, but they have the physical and mental energy demands of hard-working dogs. Create activities that utilize your dog's impressive scent following, retrieving, and carrying abilities. Constructive play is fun and also strengthens your dog's bond with you.

GAME OF "HIGH FIVE"

Cockers can be surprisingly dominant with their human families, so training your dog to sit on command and offer its paw helps reinforce that you are the natural leader. Giving a paw is in itself a submissive gesture. When children play "high five" with the dog, it learns that they too are in command.

Avoid small balls which could be swallowed

FUN WITH MOVING OBJECTS

Giving verbal encouragement, teach your Cocker to roll a ball with its nose. It is a good exercise in concentration and is a prelude to "playing football" with your dog. Avoid food rewards because they are too potent a distraction from the game. Dogs enjoy chasing a ball because it stimulates natural canine behaviour.

EXERCISE THE SCENT SENSE

Cockers have exceptional scenting abilities. Exercise this sense by showing your dog a toy, such as a rubber ball, that has a distinctive odour. While your dog is out of sight, hide the ball, then tell your dog to "Find the ball". Encourage it with an excited voice as it gets closer and a duller voice when it gets further away.

A Cocker's nose is very sensitive to smell

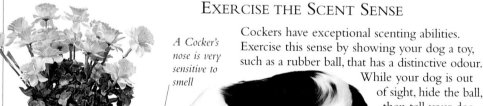

"SPEAK" AND "HUSH"

Spaniels are natural barkers. Prevent barking problems by training your dog, using food or toy rewards, to "Speak" on command. Once it has mastered barking to order, your Cocker is ready to learn to be quiet when it hears the word "Hush". Watchdog barking can then be turned on and off at your discretion.

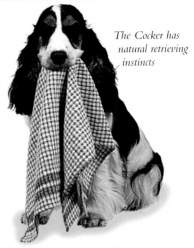

The Cocker has natural retrieving instincts

Barking could be a problem if it is not controlled

RETRIEVE ON COMMAND

This is an easy game that should come quite naturally to a breed with such strong yet gentle jaws. Using praise as your reward, train your Cocker to hold an object in its mouth, then to pick it up. Progress to teaching the command "Fetch", initially on a lead to ensure compliance. Once your dog understands the concept "Fetch", you can train it to fetch a variety of items.

TOYS BELONG TO YOU

Some Cockers are possessive of their toys and food. Train your dog from an early age to release any item, initially for food rewards, then solely to verbal commands. Play this game often to maintain authority.

THE OWNER ALWAYS WINS

Forget about democracy. You own all the toys and whenever you play with your dog, you win. After each game, make sure that your dog sees you collect all the toys and put them away. This reinforces in its mind that you are in charge. It also makes toys more valuable, useful for giving to your dog when you go out. Avoid games that are too stimulating such as tug-of-war; your Cocker might want to win so much that it forgets some of its training. Ensure that play is still satisfying by finishing all games on a positive note, with food treats, stroking, or some encouraging words.

GOOD CONTROL

LIKE ALL OTHER DOGS, your Cocker Spaniel may present you with
unexpected behaviour problems. Some Cockers are sensitive
to the unfamiliar, others may be provocative and socially
dominant. Most difficulties can be overcome through proper
care and training, and by establishing positive control.

MEETING STRANGERS

Cockers can be surprisingly dominant. If
your dog is aggressive towards strangers, ask
a friend to act as the stranger, avoiding eye
contact with the dog. Find
the distance at which your
dog shows no antagonism and
reward polite behaviour.
Reduce the distance over
several weeks. Always reinforce
your control with commands.

HAPPILY OCCUPIED ALONE

No dog enjoys being left alone, and that
includes the family-oriented Cocker Spaniel.
Exercise your dog before you go out, not
after you return; this will encourage it to rest.
Just before you leave the house, give your
Cocker its favourite toy with an added extra –
cheese spread or peanut butter placed in it.
Always leave and return without a fuss.

*Toy used as
distraction*

FRIENDLINESS WITH OTHER DOGS

A well-socialized dog will show curious
interest rather than fear or hostility when
meeting other dogs. If your Cocker gets
worried or aggressive, introduce it to a
friend's placid, even-tempered dog. Find
a distance where your dog is at ease,
and reward relaxed behaviour. Stop all
games if your dog behaves aggressively.
Over time, draw the two dogs closer
together, rewarding calmness each time.

Dog remains calm while umbrella is opened

DEALING WITH A WILFUL DOG

Cockers are delightful companions but some, solid colours in particular, can be wilful and disobedient. Be firm and use psychological rather than physical discipline, leaving its lead on while it is indoors for safe handling. If your dog does not respond, withdraw all rewards – and that includes your affection! If you are inexperienced with dogs or concerned about your Cocker's behaviour, contact your vet or local training club to arrange for obedience lessons. Most problems can be overcome when the origin is understood.

DETERRENTS FOR CHEWING

Cockers love to chew and young ones in particular can be very destructive. In your absence, provide a chewable toy to occupy your dog. To teach your dog not to chew household items, spray a potentially chewable article such as a shoe with bitter-tasting but safe aerosol and leave it near your dog. The taste will deter it from trying other items it might find.

UNFAMILIAR SITUATIONS

If your Cocker is frightened by a new sight or sound, reintroduce it to that situation when it is far enough away not to be provoked. Reward calm behaviour with treats and gentle words. Over several weeks, bring the dog closer to the object until it is no longer afraid.

Child avoids eye contact while eating ice cream

RESISTING TEMPTATION

Prevent begging by never giving food while you are eating. Relenting with the occasional titbit will actually encourage this bad behaviour more than regular offerings. If your dog begs, command it to lie down, then look away; it is a powerful form of training. The best way to avoid begging is by keeping your Cocker in another room at mealtimes. Reward your dog's obedience with approving words and play, but not food treats.

FOODS FOR YOUR DOG

DO NOT LET YOUR COCKER treat your kitchen like a local restaurant where it can choose from a lengthy daily menu – you decide what your dog eats. Select from the vast array of commercially-prepared moist or dry foods or feed home-cooked meals. Always maintain feeding routines.

CANNED FOODS

Moist, meaty canned foods come in a wide range of flavours and textures. Some are high in protein and are mixed with dry dog meal to provide added calories and vital carbohydrates; others are nutritionally complete on their own. Tinned food will only stay fresh in the bowl for a few hours.

Standard variety

Special formula for clinical conditions

"Stew" with gravy

Chunks in jelly

DRY MEAL

Crunchy dry meal is added to canned food to improve the texture, contribute fibre and fat, as well as exercise the jaws.

COMPLETE DRY FOODS

Complete dry foods are a convenient and practical way to feed Cockers, especially if you have two or more. By weight, standard brands contain about four times as many calories as tinned food. In quantity, a Cocker needs less dry food than tinned food and dog meal. Dry food produces less waste, making it easier to clean up.

HIGH-ENERGY
Puppies require nutrient-rich, easily digestible foods to sustain growth.

REGULAR
Adult formulas maintain mature dogs on a variety of activity levels.

LOW-CALORIE
Older, overweight, or sedentary dogs need less energy from their food.

TEETH-CLEANING
These large, crunchy chunks promote healthy gums and help control tartar.

Semi-moist Foods

These foods are packaged in many flavours, including cheese, and have three times the calories of canned foods. A high carbohydrate content makes semi-moist foods unsuitable for diabetic dogs. Like dry foods, they can be left out all day so your dog can eat at its own pace.

Suitable Chews

Cockers are chewers and rawhide wrapped in the shape of a bone is an excellent chew, as is a hard, compressed biscuit chew. Avoid sterilized bones, which can fracture teeth.

Rawhide chew

Treats and Biscuits

It is fun to give your Cocker snacks, but many are high in calories and being too generous with them can lead to obesity.

Use these snacks as rewards and limit the amount given. The more snacks your Cocker receives, the smaller its meals should be.

BACON-FLAVOURED   SAVOURY RINGS   MEATY CHUNKS   LIVER ROUNDS

Table Foods

In general, a diet that is well balanced for us is also nourishing for canines. Never encourage begging by feeding scraps from the table, but prepare a special portion for your dog. White meat with pasta or rice is an excellent meal, but avoid strong spices.

Medical Diets

International pet food manufacturers produce a vast range of special diets to aid in the treatment of medical conditions ranging from heart disease to obesity. Your vet can recommend the best one.

Chicken is easily digested and lower in calories than red meat

When serving, mix rice or pasta with meat to ensure it is all eaten

Dry prescription food

Moist prescription food

HEALTHY EATING

ESTABLISH SOUND EATING habits in your dog's life by feeding the right number of calories for its activity level. Some Cockers, especially neutered ones, have a natural tendency towards obesity. You can prevent this by feeding at set times, and never from your table. Always provide fresh drinking water.

DIETARY NEEDS FOR ALL AGES

GROWING PUPPY

Puppy waits patiently for signal to eat

It is important to ensure that your puppy receives plenty of the nutrients essential for healthy growth. Feed four equal portions of complete dry puppy food or semi-moist food daily. The alternative is to feed two light meals of any nutritious breakfast cereal and milk, and two portions of canned food and dog meal, or meat and pasta or rice daily. Eliminate one light meal when the puppy is 12 weeks old and another at six months.

Serve food at room temperature, never straight from the refrigerator

FEEDING REQUIREMENTS

These figures are only a guide – each dog has its own precise nutritional needs, and different foods vary in calories. Your vet can give you specific advice for your Cocker.

DAILY ENERGY DEMANDS FOR COCKER SPANIELS

AGE	WEIGHT	CALORIES	DRY FOOD	SEMI-MOIST	CANNED/MEAL
2 MONTHS	2.6 kg (5.7 lb)	590	176 g (6 oz)	196 g (7 oz)	295 g/100 g (10½ oz/3½ oz)
3 MONTHS	5 kg (11 lb)	795	238 g (8½ oz)	265 g (9½ oz)	398 g/135 g (14 oz/5 oz)
6 MONTHS	8.8 kg (19.4 lb)	895	268 g (9½ oz)	298 g (10½ oz)	448 g/152 g (16 oz/5½ oz)
TYPICAL ADULT	9–16 kg (20–35 lb)	570–880	170–263 g (6–9 oz)	190–293 g (6½–10½ oz)	285–440 g/97–150 g (10–15½ oz/3½–5½ oz)
ACTIVE ADULT	9–16 kg (20–35 lb)	650–1,000	194–299 g (7–10½ oz)	216–333 g (7½–11½ oz)	325–500 g/111–170 g (11½–17½ oz/4–6 oz)
VERY ACTIVE ADULT	9–16 kg (20–35 lb)	910–1,400	272–419 g (9½–14½ oz)	303–466 g (10½–16½ oz)	455–700 g/155–238 g (16–24½ oz/5½–8½ oz)
ELDERLY (10 YEARS+)	9–16 kg (20–35 lb)	520–800	155–239 g (5½–8½ oz)	173–266 g (6–9½ oz)	260–400 g/88–136 g (9–14 oz/3–5 oz)

MATURE ADULT

The energy requirements of the adult Cocker vary greatly and depend upon a number of factors: level of activity, health, and temperament. Sedentary, indoor dogs are more prone to weight gain. As a rule, feed once or twice a day.

ELDERLY COCKER

Older dogs generally have lower energy demands and should either be fed smaller portions or switched over to less energy-dense foods. Reduced protein intake prolongs the working life of the kidneys.

FEEDING ROUTINES

By establishing a strict routine at mealtimes, your Cocker will recognize that you are the boss. Train your dog to sit and stay, even in the presence of food, then to eat when released from the command. Offer food to a puppy from your hand and stroke it while it is eating. This reduces the risk of it guarding its food.

Use body language to reinforce that you are in command of your dog's feeding habits

DAILY ENERGY DEMANDS FOR AMERICAN COCKER SPANIELS

AGE	WEIGHT	CALORIES	DRY FOOD	SEMI-MOIST	CANNED/MEAL
2 MONTHS	2 kg (4.4 lb)	570	170 g (6 oz)	190 g (7 oz)	285 g/97 g (10 oz/3½ oz)
3 MONTHS	4 kg (8.8 lb)	670	200 g (7 oz)	223 g (8 oz)	335 g/114 g (12 oz/4 oz)
6 MONTHS	8.2 kg (18 lb)	785	235 g (8½ oz)	261 g (9 oz)	392 g/133 g (14 oz/4½ oz)
TYPICAL ADULT	9–15 kg (20–33 lb)	570–840	170–251 g (6–9 oz)	190–280 g (6½–10 oz)	285–420 g/97–143 g (10–15 oz/3½–5 oz)
ACTIVE ADULT	9–15 kg (20–33 lb)	650–955	194–286 g (7–10 oz)	216–318 g (7½–11 oz)	325–478 g/111–162 g (11½–17 oz/4–5½ oz)
VERY ACTIVE ADULT	9–15 kg (20–33 lb)	910–1,335	272–399 g (9½–14 oz)	303–445 g (10½–15½ oz)	455–668 g/155–227 g (16–23½ oz/5½–8 oz)
ELDERLY (10 YEARS+)	9–15 kg (20–33 lb)	520–800	155–239 g (5½–8½ oz)	173–266 g (6–9½ oz)	260–400 g/88–136 g (9–14 oz/3–5 oz)

BASIC BODY CARE

THEIR DENSE COATS, lopped ears, and relatively loose skin, mean that Cocker Spaniels need more routine body care than most other breeds. Regular body maintenance reduces the likelihood of veterinary attention at a later stage. Examine carefully and, if necessary, clean all body openings daily.

ENSURING CLEAR, HEALTHY EYES

Dampen cotton wool with tepid salt water

Healthy eyes are bright and sparkling with dull pink mucous membranes, but with age Cockers develop droopy lower eyelids where mucous and debris accumulate. Clean the area around the eyes daily with cotton wool moistened with tepid salt water. If there is a green or yellow discharge, or if the eyes are bloodshot or cloudy, arrange for a veterinary examination.

CLEANING THE LIP FOLDS

Pull back the top lip and clean lower fold

Cockers have a slight fold of skin in their lower lips in which food accumulates, leading to possible infection. Clean the folds after each meal with damp cotton wool. Chronic infections need surgical removal of the fold.

PREVENT TOOTH TARTAR

Without weekly cleaning, tartar can collect on the teeth, leading to bad breath, root infection, and gum disease. Avoid human toothpaste, which froths and will be swallowed. In addition to regular professional scaling and polishing, rawhide chews are helpful in controlling tartar build-up. This dog's teeth and gums require medical attention.

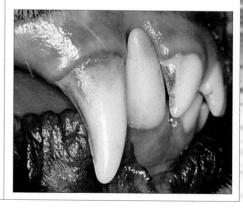

INSPECTING THE EARS

Heavy, drooping ears can lead to wax build-up and infection. Check for wax, inflammation, odour, and foreign objects such as grass seeds. Remove wax with tissue, taking care not to probe too deeply into the ear.

WASHING THE PAWS

Mud cakes between the Cocker's pads and in the feathering on the legs and belly. Wash the paws in a bowl filled with tepid to cool water. Rub your fingers between the pads to remove hardened mud. Use a mild soap suitable for human skin, and always rinse and dry the paws thoroughly afterwards.

CUTTING THE NAILS

No dog likes its nails cut. Command your Cocker to sit and use a non-crushing "guillotine" clipper rather than a crushing "pliers" type to cut the tip of the nail. Light-coated dogs have light nails in which the quick is visible. For dark-nailed dogs, seek professional advice on where to make the cut.

WHERE TO CLIP NAILS
The sensitive pink area, called the quick or nail bed, contains vessels and nerves. Always cut in front of the quick. This cannot be seen in black nails, so ask your vet if you are unsure.

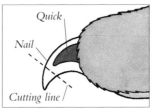

Quick

Nail

Cutting line

ANAL HYGIENE

Excessive licking or dragging of the rear can mean that the scent-producing anal sacs are blocked, causing discomfort. Wearing protective gloves, squeeze the sacs empty, applying firm pressure from both sides. Use absorbent material to collect the fluid.

MAINTAINING THE COAT

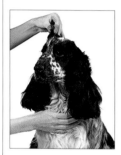

ALTHOUGH YOUR COCKER SPANIEL'S coat is one of its most appealing features, it will need constant attention if it is to remain healthy and attractive. Groom daily, even more frequently during moults, and bathe your Cocker regularly to keep possible skin problems under control.

ROUTINE GROOMING FOR COCKER SPANIELS

STRIPPING THE HEAD
Command your Cocker to sit. Brush through and then hand-strip the hair on the head with rubber thimbles. Cockers are prone to skin irritation, so check for parasites, dandruff, and signs of inflammation while grooming.

Groom daily to assert authority over your Cocker Spaniel

TRIMMING THE TAIL
With a slicker brush and then a comb, brush out tangles, dead hair, and debris from the feathering on the tail. Using scissors, trim the hair, which is susceptible to matting on the tail and around the anus.

TRIMMING THE PAWS
Cockers have deep crevices between their toes. If the hair has grown long between the toes, trim it with blunt-ended scissors. This will help prevent foreign bodies such as grass seeds from lodging painfully in the paws.

BRUSHING THE BODY
Use a slicker brush daily to massage the skin and remove dead hair from your dog's short body coat. Finish with a chamois to add extra sheen. Establish grooming early as part of obedience training.

TRIMMING THE LEGS

Brush through the feathering on the legs to remove any tangles and then cut the hair in a straight line. Cockers have very dense coats, so unless regular grooming is applied, the coat will matt. If left for too long, the tangles will become so thick that the coat will have to be shorn off.

Inspect the ears for foreign matter after your dog has played outdoors

SPECIAL ATTENTION TO THE EARS

Dense hair on the ears can weigh them down and promote a build-up of wax. The ear leather is fairly thin, so use a gentle bristle brush to remove tangles of dead hair. Thin excess hair with thinning scissors.

BATHING YOUR DOG

Avoid getting soap in the dog's eyes

2 Squeeze off excess water while your dog is still in the bath. Drape a bath towel over it and let it shake. Avoid draughts while towel drying. If you use a hair dryer, avoid hot settings. Now is the best time to cut the nails while they are softened. Groom after bathing to remove loosened hair and once more finish with words of praise.

1 People are more often allergic to Cockers than other breeds because dander builds up to a higher level in their dense coats. Shampoo all parts of your dog's body as often as necessary with a product recommended by your vet. Do not shampoo near the eyes or let water enter the ears. Clean the face with a cloth. Rinse off all shampoo thoroughly, especially under the elbows and between the hind legs.

BASIC HEALTH

YOUR COCKER DEPENDS on you for its good health. Since it cannot tell you that something is wrong, you must observe how your dog moves and behaves; any changes in activity or regular habits may be warning signs of problems. Arrange annual check-ups, and always use your veterinarian as a source of advice.

ACTIVE AND ALERT?

Cockers rarely complain. They cannot tell you if they are uncomfortable, so it is up to you to keep an eye on your dog's movements and note any changes. Watch out for any behaviour or mood alterations. While age slows down all dogs, there are also medical reasons for changes in your dog's behaviour; pain, poor circulation, or neurological problems can all be contributing factors. If your dog is not behaving as you would expect, call your veterinarian and explain what is happening.

SOUND APPETITE AND EATING HABITS

Eating and toilet routines adopted during puppyhood are normally maintained throughout life and should remain constant. Even slight changes can be a sign of ill health, and should be referred to your vet. A reduced appetite can simply indicate boredom, but may also signal illness. Asking for food but not eating it can mean tooth pain. So too can sloppy eating – with food being dropped, then picked up and eaten. A heightened appetite without weight gain can indicate a thyroid problem. Increased thirst is always important and may be a sign of infection or conditions such as diabetes and liver or kidney disease. Seek veterinary advice if your dog starts to drink excessively or develops chronic diarrhoea or constipation.

Excessive drinking may be medically significant

REGULAR PREVENTATIVE CHECKS

Cockers that are vaccinated, treated for heart worms if present, and checked annually by a veterinarian, tend to live longer than those that are not. Many conditions, such as kidney and liver disease, are not outwardly apparent, but may be diagnosed from blood samples. Problems are easiest to treat if detected early. Your vet wants you as a client and is the best source for information about your dog.

EASY MOVEMENT

Vet uses stethoscope to check the heart and lungs

Cockers walk, trot, run, and gallop with ear-waving joy and fluid ease. Your dog should be able to lie down and arise without difficulty. Be alert to any signs of discomfort. Neck and back pain can develop, especially in middle-aged dogs. Watch for an arched walk or signs of difficulty getting up or lying down. Head bobbing while walking usually means pain, as does limping.

MAKING VISITS TO THE VET FUN

Take your Cocker to the vet before it needs any treatment, so that it can have an investigative sniff and explore the premises. Ask your vet to give your dog a food treat while it is there, to make the next visit more appealing. Repeat trips can be made less of a hardship for you, too, by taking out insurance cover on your pet's health. This guarantees that the most sophisticated diagnostics and treatments will always be available without financial worry.

CARING FOR THE ELDERLY DOG

Your Cocker will not remain puppy-like forever. With age, it may become hard of hearing, its vision may deteriorate, and it will slow down. Be patient with its behaviour, and gentle in your handling. Create less physically demanding activities; older dogs still enjoy playing, but are less agile and energetic. Mental stimulation is the best antidote to ageing.

COMMON PROBLEMS

REGARDLESS OF BREED, irritating skin conditions are the most common canine medical problems treated by vets, accounting for up to 40 per cent of all clinic visits. Good hygiene, together with parasite control measures, helps to reduce the incidence and severity of these and many other common problems.

PARASITES

Parasites are an occupational hazard but are simple to control. Check your dog's coat for ticks, fleas, or mange, all of which cause skin irritation.

FLEAS AND TICKS
The flea is the most common skin parasite, followed by the tick. Use parasite control methods as recommended by your vet.

INTERNAL PARASITES
Roundworms, hookworms, tapeworms, and whipworms find homes in the dog's intestines; heart and lung worms affect those organs. Prevent rather than treat.

OBVIOUS SIGNS OF DISCOMFORT

Chronic scratching does not always indicate fleas

Paws may also be chewed in response to irritation

SCRATCHING
Dogs scratch themselves because of parasites, allergies, injuries, and other less common conditions. In Cockers, this leads to an above-average incidence of moist skin infection, called summer dermatitis or "hot spots". These unpleasant, smelly sores enlarge rapidly, and need to be cleaned thoroughly with disinfectant.

Leg is groomed excessively and may in turn become infected

PERSISTENT LICKING
All dogs like to lick themselves and some Cockers may do so obsessively, causing skin inflammation and hair loss. Anal licking is another problem; the Cocker's anal sacs become blocked and this leads to constant licking or bottom dragging. Your vet will show you how to express the sacs.

TYPICAL CANINE COMPLAINTS

With any breed, many health problems can be prevented, a better and cheaper option than having to treat complaints. Routinely examine your dog's skin, especially the ears and between the toes. Shampoo and trim the coat regularly and check teeth and gums on a weekly basis. Keep an eye on your dog's weight to avoid potential obesity.

TOOTH CHIPS AND FRACTURES

Cockers enjoy chewing sticks, bones, and even stones. Although their jaws are very strong, chewing can chip or fracture teeth and cause subsequent pain when eating. Gnawing sticks can cause mouth lacerations.

EAR DISORDERS

Air does not flow freely under the Cocker's drooping ears; increased humidity in the ear increases wax build-up, odour, and infection. Check routinely for unpleasant smell or inflammation and use wax removers preventatively as recommended by your vet.

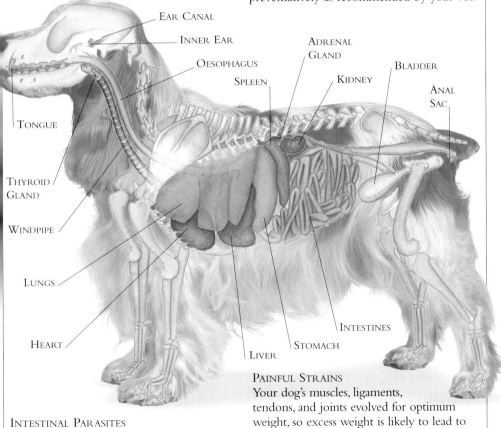

EAR CANAL

INNER EAR

OESOPHAGUS

SPLEEN

ADRENAL GLAND

KIDNEY

BLADDER

ANAL SAC

TONGUE

THYROID GLAND

WINDPIPE

LUNGS

HEART

INTESTINES

STOMACH

LIVER

INTESTINAL PARASITES

Worms and other parasites such as *Giardia* and *Coccidia* cause diarrhoea, with mucus and blood, and sometimes vomiting. Lung and heart worms reduce exercise tolerance.

PAINFUL STRAINS

Your dog's muscles, ligaments, tendons, and joints evolved for optimum weight, so excess weight is likely to lead to injuries. The most common serious injury is torn knee ligaments and occurs in overweight Cockers over eight years old; surgery is required to repair the damage.

BREED-SPECIFIC PROBLEMS

SELECTIVE BREEDING for desirable traits also concentrates potentially harmful genes, and Cocker Spaniels may suffer from a variety of inherited problems. The most common involve the eyes, kidneys, skin, hip joints, and brain. Testing stock for hereditary disorders helps to ensure healthy offspring.

HEREDITARY EYE DISEASES

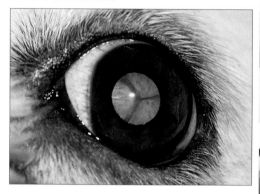

HEREDITARY CATARACTS
American Cocker Spaniels can develop a hereditary form of cataracts at any time in their lives from the age of one. Healthy eyes are transparent, but a dog with cataracts has cloudy eyes with lenses that turn crystalline. Cocker Spaniels do not suffer from this hereditary condition. Under certain clinical conditions cataracts can be removed and vision partly restored. Plastic lenses are sometimes inserted to improve restored vision even further.

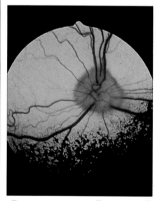
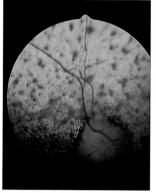

GLAUCOMA AND RETINAL DISEASE
Both types of Cocker can suffer from glaucoma, a painful increase in pressure within the eye, and from progressive retinal atrophy (PRA), a disease of the retina at the back of the eye. Healthy retinas *(above, left)* have a generous blood supply, while atrophic retinas *(above, right)* have fewer and thinner blood vessels. This condition, where the retina slowly "dies", affects Cockers over five years old. American Cockers develop a generalized form of PRA, while Cockers develop a milder form that does not always lead to blindness.

IMPORTANCE OF HEALTH SCREENING

Responsible Cocker Spaniel breeders have their stock examined for the presence of hereditary eye conditions such as PRA and cataracts. These breeders will be able to give you copies of all appropriate eye screening certificates – especially important if you are thinking about owning an American Cocker. When acquiring a puppy, ask to see both parents; this will give you a better idea of its potential adult temperament as well as its colour when it matures. In the future it will be possible to use DNA "fingerprinting" on tiny blood samples to determine whether an individual carries genes of a potentially devastating inherited disease.

OTHER DISORDERS MORE COMMON IN COCKER SPANIELS

Although Cocker Spaniels are physically robust dogs with sound physiques, they are more susceptible than average to a number of inherited medical conditions. These can only be prevented through careful breeding. Seek medical attention if problems develop.

EPILEPSY
Epilepsy occurs occasionally, but is more frequent in the offspring of epileptic dogs. Fits range from the very mild to violent with unconsciousness. Always contact your vet.

HIP DYSPLASIA
Although more common in large breeds, hip dysplasia does affect some Cockers. The hips appear fine at birth but by two years of age it is evident that the ball of the femur does not fit well in the socket of the hip; any movement causes pain. Diagnosed by X-ray, treatment may involve medication.

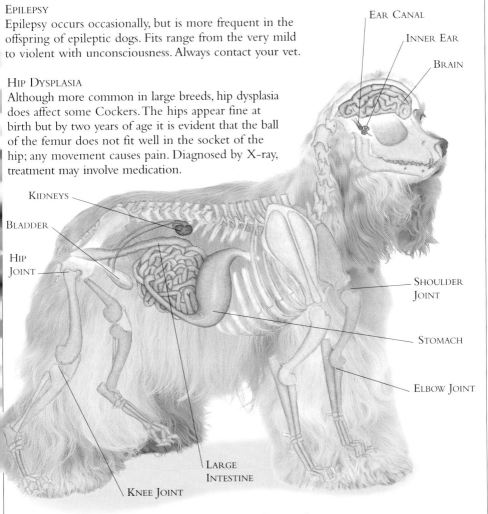

EAR CANAL

INNER EAR

BRAIN

KIDNEYS

BLADDER

HIP JOINT

SHOULDER JOINT

STOMACH

ELBOW JOINT

LARGE INTESTINE

KNEE JOINT

KIDNEY CONDITIONS
Cockers suffer from two forms of inherited kidney disease where the kidneys do not grow properly: familial nephropathy and renal cortical hypoplasia. Affected dogs do not live to more than a few years of age.

SMELLY SKIN
Many Cockers develop a skin condition called seborrhea, where the sebaceous glands over-secrete. The result is a distinctive musty odour and a predisposition to bacterial skin disease. Routine shampooing is necessary.

FORESEEING DANGERS

COCKER SPANIELS LOVE LIFE and have an inclination to act first and think later. Monitor your dog's activities, especially outdoors, and never leave it alone where, through boredom or curiosity, it may put itself in peril. Remember that dog fatalities are caused by cars more than anything else.

ENSURING SAFETY WITH YOUR COCKER SPANIEL

INSTILLING ROAD SENSE

Cockers are naturally enthusiastic dogs – even the best-trained individual may dart out onto a road if it is excited or worried. Walk your dog on a lead wherever potential dangers exist. If a driver swerves to avoid your dog, any damage to the car may be your legal responsibility and could turn into a costly incident. It is wise to insure yourself for liability against your dog's activities.

POTENTIAL HAZARDS IN WATER

Although Cockers love water, their heavy coats can impair safety. Prevent your dog from swimming where you would not swim and ensure that it can get out after it jumps in. Icy water causes hypothermia, so should be avoided. Be wary of water-borne diseases such as leptospirosis, spread by infected rat urine, or blue-green algae bloom, which may cause itchy skin, diarrhoea, and even death.

CONTROLLING AN INQUISITIVE NATURE

Monitor your Cocker carefully when it is off the lead. Adventurous, curious dogs are prone to injury, and exploratory wanders or investigative digging can result in bites from wild animals, stings, and irritations caused by plants or insects. Keep your dog away from known dangers, and always carry a basic first-aid kit to treat minor cuts and lacerations before the injuries can be seen by a vet.

COMMON POISONS AND CONTAMINANTS

IF INGESTED		ACTION
Slug and snail bait Strychnine rat poison Illegal drugs Aspirin and other painkillers Sedatives and antidepressants	Warfarin rat poison Lead (batteries, etc.) Antifreeze	Examine any packaging to determine its contents. If the poison was swallowed within the last two hours, induce vomiting by giving crystals of washing soda, a "ball" of wet salt, or 3 per cent hydrogen peroxide by mouth. Consult your vet immediately.
Caustic soda Dishwasher granules Paint remover or thinner Kerosene or petrol Drain, toilet, or oven cleaner	Chlorine bleach Laundry detergents Wood preservatives Polishes	Do not induce vomiting. Give raw egg white, bicarbonate of soda, charcoal powder, or olive oil by mouth. Apply a paste of bicarbonate of soda to any burns in the mouth. Seek urgent medical advice from your veterinarian.

IF IN CONTACT WITH THE COAT	ACTION
Paint Tar Petroleum products Motor oil	Do not apply paint remover or concentrated biological detergents. Wearing protective gloves, rub plenty of liquid paraffin or vegetable oil into the coat. Bathe with warm, soapy water or baby shampoo. Rub in flour to help absorb the poison.
Anything other than paint, tar, petroleum products, and motor oil	Wearing protective gloves, flush the affected area for at least five minutes, using plenty of clean, tepid water. Then bathe the contaminated coat thoroughly with warm, soapy water or mild, non-irritating baby shampoo.

EMERGENCY TREATMENT

With any case of poisoning, look for signs of shock, and give essential first aid as required. Contact your vet or local poison-control centre for specific advice, and begin home treatment as quickly as possible, preferably under professional guidance by telephone.

PROTECTING YOUR DOG

Empty containers should not be given as toys

Cockers are naturally curious and will chew anything. Keep all household and garden chemicals away from your dog and never give an empty container as a chew toy. Switch off electrical sockets when not in use and spray visible cords with bitter-tasting aerosol.

PREVENT SCAVENGING

Scavenging is part of natural Cocker behaviour, but it can lead to medical emergencies. Train your dog to "Drop" on command and prevent it from eating other animals' droppings. Worm regularly according to your vet's advice. Do not feed bones to your Cocker – soft bones in particular are easily swallowed and can block the intestines, sometimes necessitating surgery.

EMERGENCY FIRST AID

A HOME FIRST-AID KIT contains all the items needed for patching up minor injuries. More serious emergencies are much less common, but with an understanding of basic principles and techniques such as artificial respiration and cardiac massage, you could save your dog's life.

FIRST-AID PRINCIPLES AND BASIC EQUIPMENT

The fundamentals of human first aid also apply to dogs. Your objectives are to preserve life, prevent further injury, control damage, minimize pain and distress, promote healing, and get your dog safely to a veterinarian for professional care. Have a fully-stocked first-aid kit handy and use it to treat minor wounds, once you are certain there are no more serious, life-threatening problems to deal with.

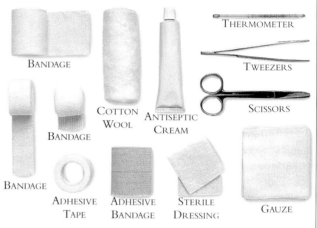

THERMOMETER

BANDAGE

TWEEZERS

SCISSORS

COTTON WOOL

ANTISEPTIC CREAM

BANDAGE

BANDAGE

ADHESIVE TAPE

ADHESIVE BANDAGE

STERILE DRESSING

GAUZE

HOW TO ASSESS AN UNCONSCIOUS DOG

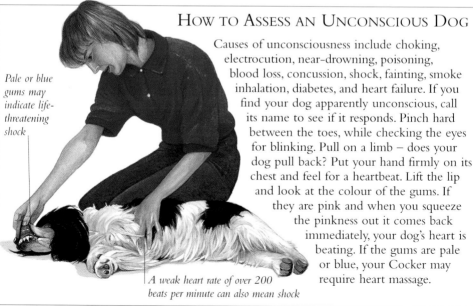

Causes of unconsciousness include choking, electrocution, near-drowning, poisoning, blood loss, concussion, shock, fainting, smoke inhalation, diabetes, and heart failure. If you find your dog apparently unconscious, call its name to see if it responds. Pinch hard between the toes, while checking the eyes for blinking. Pull on a limb – does your dog pull back? Put your hand firmly on its chest and feel for a heartbeat. Lift the lip and look at the colour of the gums. If they are pink and when you squeeze the pinkness out it comes back immediately, your dog's heart is beating. If the gums are pale or blue, your Cocker may require heart massage.

Pale or blue gums may indicate life-threatening shock

A weak heart rate of over 200 beats per minute can also mean shock

Artificial Respiration and Cardiac Massage

Do not attempt to give artificial respiration or heart massage unless your dog is unconscious and will die without your help. If your dog has been pulled from water, suspend it by its hind legs for at least 30 seconds to drain the air passages. If it has been electrocuted, do not touch it until the electricity is turned off. If it has choked, press forcefully over the ribs to dislodge the object. Never put yourself at risk; if possible, share first-aid procedures with someone else or have them telephone the nearest veterinarian and arrange transport.

Hold muzzle shut and seal your mouth over dog's nostrils

Tongue pulled forwards and debris removed

1 Place your dog on its side, with its head slightly lower than the rest of its body, to send more blood to the brain. Clear the airway by straightening the neck, pulling the tongue forwards, and sweeping the mouth with two fingers to remove any saliva or obstructions. Also ensure that the nose is not clogged with mucus or debris.

2 Close the mouth, hold the muzzle with both hands, and place your mouth around the nose. Blow in until you see the chest expand, then let the lungs deflate. Repeat this procedure 10–20 times per minute, checking the pulse every 10 seconds to make sure the heart is beating.

Pumping forces blood towards brain

3 If the heart has stopped, begin cardiac massage immediately. With the dog still on its side, place the heel of one hand on the left side of the chest just behind the elbow, then the heel of your other hand on top. Press vigorously down and forwards to push blood into the brain, pumping 80–100 times per minute. Alternate 20–25 cardiac massages with 10 seconds of mouth-to-nose respiration until the heart beats, then continue resuscitation until breathing starts.

Always Look for Shock

Shock is a potentially life-endangering condition which occurs when the body's circulation fails. It can be caused by vomiting, diarrhoea, poisons, animal bites, a twisted stomach, bleeding, and many other illnesses or accidents, and onset may not be apparent for several hours. The signs include pale or blue gums, rapid breathing, a faint or quickened pulse, cold extremities, and general weakness. Treating shock takes precedence over other injuries, including fractures. Your priorities are to control any bleeding, maintain body heat, and support vital functions. Unless shock is the result of heatstroke, wrap your dog loosely in a warm blanket, elevate its hindquarters, stabilize breathing and the heart if necessary, and get immediate medical advice. If your dog begins to panic, try to prevent it from injuring itself further, and be careful not to get bitten.

MINOR INJURY AND ILLNESS

A BASIC KNOWLEDGE OF how to administer medicines and other simple treatment is valuable for owners in case their dog has an accident or becomes ill. Learn how to improvise a muzzle and bandage wounds until a vet is called. The most common Cocker injuries are grass seeds in the ears or paws, cut pads, and bites.

APPLYING AN EMERGENCY BANDAGE TO THE EAR

Assistant applies pressure to the wound

2 While your assistant holds the absorbent pad in place, slip the tights over your dog's head. This will hold the ear firmly, helping the blood to clot. Ensure that the windpipe receives no undue pressure.

1 With an assistant on hand to steady your dog, apply clean, preferably non-stick, absorbent material to the wound. Take care you are not bitten through fright. Cut a section from a pair of tights and slip it over your hands.

BANDAGING A WOUNDED PAW

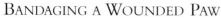

Ask an assistant to support your dog from behind. Apply a fresh, absorbent pad to the cut, wrap the pad in place with stretchy gauze, and secure the dressing with clinging stretch or adhesive bandage. Consult your vet about antibiotics or possible surgery. Change bandages daily to reduce the risk of infection.

Assistant kneels behind, keeping injured dog still

3 The tights prevent the wounded ear from flapping. If necessary, secure the tights at each end with tape to prevent your dog from removing the bandage with its paws. Visit your vet as soon as possible for examination of the wound.

IMPROVISING A MUZZLE

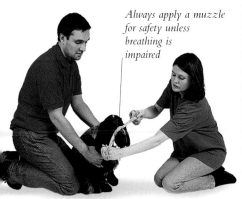

Always apply a muzzle for safety unless breathing is impaired

1 Cockers may bite if in pain so, unless there are breathing problems, apply a muzzle before you examine an injured area. With the help of an assistant, make a loop of soft material and slip it over the muzzle.

2 With the loop in place, tighten it gently. Then bring both lengths of material down and cross them under the jaws. If your dog is confused or upset, speak to it in a relaxed, comforting tone as you proceed.

3 To complete the process, wrap the material around the back of the ears and tie the ends securely in a knot. This holds the muzzle firmly in place and allows you to examine and treat the injured area.

ADMINISTERING MEDICINES

Pill can be hidden in food

GIVING A PILL
With your dog seated, open its mouth and insert the pill as far back as possible. Then hold the jaw shut and tilt it upwards, stroking the neck to induce swallowing.

GIVING LIQUIDS
If mixing in food is not practical, use a syringe to squirt the medicine into the mouth, not the throat where it may enter the windpipe. Hold the muzzle shut until your dog swallows.

REMOVING FOREIGN OBJECTS

Check your Cocker's hair for grass seeds and other vegetable matter, especially between the toes, in the ears, and around the vulva in females. Use your fingers or a pair of tweezers to remove these foreign objects before they penetrate so deeply into the skin that veterinary attention is required to extricate them.

EARLY BREED ORIGINS

SPANIELS HAVE BEEN OUR companions in the field and by the fireside for at least 1,000 years. Their exact origins are lost in time, although their name suggests that they spread out into the rest of Europe from the Iberian peninsula. It was not until 100 years ago that modern spaniel classifications were developed.

HISTORY OF THE COCKER SPANIEL

HISTORICAL REFERENCES

The earliest known use of the term "Spaniel" is found in the Ancient Welsh Laws compiled by King Howell the Good in AD 914. In the 1300s, both Geoffrey Chaucer in Great Britain and Gaston de Foix in France described spaniel personalities much as they are today. By the 1500s, the Cocker Spaniel's ancestors were spread throughout much of Europe, working with the hawker, hawk, and net.

WORKING TO THE GUN

With the arrival of the gun, hunters now needed spaniels with shorter legs than the Water Spaniels; this led to the development of the modern Cocker. Breeders crossed different types of spaniel to achieve breeds that could flush out different types of bird. So, "cocking" spaniels were developed to aid hunters who tracked woodcock.

HUNTER AND SPANIEL

EARLY HAWKING ROLE
Hawks prevented game birds from flying away, spaniels (the size of modern setters) scented them, and hunters captured the birds in nets.

DISTANT RELATIVES

Spaniels spread throughout Europe – to countries that included France, Portugal, Germany, and The Netherlands – where they evolved regionally to suit the needs of local sportsmen. In this century, English Cocker and Springer Spaniels have been used to revitalize European relatives driven to near extinction by war or neglect. Indeed, a number of these old gundog breeds have enjoyed something of a revival in recent years, in particular the Small Münsterländer.

SMALL MÜNSTERLÄNDER
Small pointer retriever developed in Germany from descendants of hawking spaniels

DUTCH PARTRIDGE DOG
*Descendant of ancient Dutch breed used
in Middle Ages to catch partridge and
pheasant by net*

PORTUGUESE WATER DOG
*Probable ancestor of extinct
English and modern Irish
Water Spaniels*

EPAGNEUL PONT–AUDEMER
*Water dog developed in Normandy, France, in the
1600s from the larger French Spaniel and still used
like the Cocker to flush game*

BRITTANY
*Ancient French hunter, pointer,
and retriever, revived from near
extinction earlier this century*

**NOVA SCOTIA DUCK
TOLLING RETRIEVER**
*Canadian descendant of English
"decoy" dogs used to draw ducks
close to hunters*

RECENT HISTORY

WHILE SPANIEL BREEDS thrived throughout Europe, they were most successful in Britain, where they served the hunter and acted as faithful companions. Land or Field Spaniels were divided by weight; larger individuals were called Springers, while those under 11.3 kg (25 lb) were known as Cockers.

DEVELOPMENT OF THE BREED

LAND AND WATER SPANIELS

Up until the 1700s, all gundogs in Britain were classified as Land or Water Spaniels, according to the terrain they worked best. Water Spaniels included the Irish Water Spaniel and its now extinct English cousin. The Land Spaniel group was in turn subdivided, with the largest individuals evolving to become setters and retrievers, and the smaller breeds retaining their original spaniel name. By the 19th century, all spaniels were grouped under the title Field Spaniels.

EARLY SPANIELS IN THE FIELD

COCKERS AND SPRINGERS

Although the name "Cocker" was used for the first time at a dog show in Birmingham, England, in 1859, Cockers or "flushers" continued to be shown as Field Spaniels until 1892, when the division between Cockers and Springers was made. The breed's history really began in 1879, with the birth of Obo; this black Cocker was the dog from whom all modern Cockers can trace their lineage.

OBO – THE FIRST MODERN COCKER

RED BRUCIE

AMERICAN COCKER ORIGINS

In 1882, F.F. Pitcher, a breeder from New England, USA, imported Chloe II, pregnant by Obo. In her litter was Obo II, the dog credited as the source of both types of Cocker in the United States. In 1921, Herman Mellenthin bred Red Brucie who, along with his descendents, established the American Cocker Spaniel as it is today. By the late 1920s, selective breeding saw the emergence of a distinct new Cocker, with the most obvious difference from its English cousin being in the shape of its head.

BRITISH RELATIVES

The Cocker's British cousins vary dramatically in size, from the tiny, companionable King Charles to the bulky, almost mastiff-like Clumber. All share similar origins and common temperament characteristics.

CLUMBER SPANIEL
Named after the Duke of Newcastle's Clumber Park. May have Alpine blood

SPRINGER SPANIEL
Heavier than the Cocker, but shares its cheery disposition

CAVALIER KING CHARLES SPANIEL
Breed developed early this century to imitate the dogs in 17th-century paintings by Van Dyck

SUSSEX SPANIEL
Now quite rare, this game-tracking breed was recreated this century from diminished stock

KING CHARLES SPANIEL
Toy Spaniel popularized by King Charles II in the late 1600s

FIELD SPANIEL
A rare British Land Spaniel, lower to the ground and longer in body than both Cockers and Springers

WELSH SPRINGER SPANIEL
Closest to the Cocker in both size and merry nature. This active dog is used by authorities to scent out contraband

REPRODUCTION

COCKER SPANIELS HAVE few fertility problems and produce litters of between five and eight puppies. Experienced individuals mate easily, but inexperienced dogs often need assistance. Consider breeding your dog only after discussing it with your vet. Ensure that homes will be available for the entire litter.

THE MATING INSTINCT

Healthy males as young as 10 months old can be used for mating. It is best to wait until a female is about two years old, in roughly her third oestrous cycle, when she is emotionally prepared for a litter. A bitch's cycle varies considerably, but generally speaking ovulation occurs 10-12 days after the first sign of bleeding and vulvar swelling. The most successful matings are most likely to take place on the male's home turf.

PREGNANCY DIAGNOSIS

Ovulation, the optimum time to mate, is accurately indicated by an increased level of the hormone progesterone in the blood. Pregnancy, however, cannot be confirmed by blood or urine tests. Ultrasound at three weeks or a physical examination slightly later remain the best means of diagnosis.

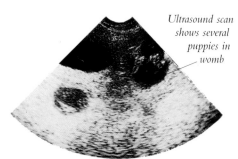

Ultrasound scan shows several puppies in womb

DEALING WITH MISMATING

Mismatings can be avoided by keeping a watchful eye on your bitch when in season, by using tablets or injections to prevent ovulation, or by spaying. If an unwanted mating does occur, contact your vet. A pregnancy can be terminated, usually within three days of mating, with a hormone injection. This will induce an immediate repeat season, demanding renewed vigilance for 8–15 days after the beginning of vaginal discharge.

SPECIAL NEEDS OF AN EXPECTANT BITCH

During the first month of pregnancy, your bitch should continue to exercise freely. Thereafter, the increasing weight of the litter will naturally make her slower and less agile. Swimming is good exercise, but avoid cold water. After the sixth week, food intake should be gradually increased, so that by the expected delivery date the bitch will be eating 30 per cent more than usual. Provide a proper balance of calcium and phosphorus in the diet to promote strong bone growth.

MALE AND FEMALE REPRODUCTIVE SYSTEMS

A bitch comes into season twice yearly, is fertile for three days during each cycle, and will be receptive to mating only during these periods. Males, however, willingly mate all year round. For the female, ovulation continues throughout life and there is no menopause, although breeding in later years is risky. Pregnancy lasts for about 63 days.

RESPONSIBLE BREEDING

If planning to breed your Cocker, seek professional advice from your vet or from an experienced and reputable breeder. Ensure that the prospective parents' physical and emotional attributes will enhance the breed. Both should have their blood lines checked for kidney disease, eyes examined for inherited diseases, and, if your vet feels it is appropriate, their hips X-rayed for hip dysplasia. Ask your vet whether your dog should be tested for brucellosis (a canine venereal disease) before mating. Remember that it is your responsibility to find each of the offspring a safe home.

PREVENTING PREGNANCY

Neutering is the most effective and safest means of preventing pregnancy. The female, because she carries the young, is the usual candidate. Both the ovaries and the uterus are removed, followed by a week's rest. The male operation is easier; a small incision is made in the scrotum to remove the testicles.

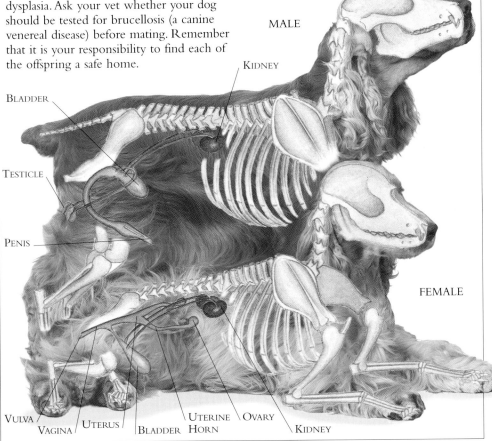

MALE

KIDNEY

BLADDER

TESTICLE

PENIS

FEMALE

VULVA

VAGINA UTERUS

BLADDER

UTERINE HORN

OVARY

KIDNEY

PRE- AND POST-WHELPING

SEVERAL WEEKS BEFORE labour is due to begin, introduce the expectant mother to her whelping box and arrange for your vet to be available in case of problems. Although most Cockers seldom have difficulties, it is best to have experienced help both at the delivery and later, for after-care of weak puppies.

INTRODUCING A WHELPING BOX

Introduce the mother-to-be to her whelping box at least two weeks before her expected delivery. The box should be at least 80 cm (31 in) long and deep, and made of plywood to prevent damage from birth fluids. The three sides should be 25–30 cm (10–12 in) high to prevent the puppies from escaping, and the fourth side half this height to allow the mother to get in and out easily. Start collecting newspaper; you will need bundles of it to line the box and to act as bedding for the puppies for the next two months.

DELIVERY CARE

If you have never been present at a birth, ask an experienced dog breeder to attend, and inform your vet when labour begins. Keep the room temperature at around 25° C (77° F). If after two hours your bitch does not produce a puppy, contact your vet once again for advice. The puppy's position may need manipulating to facilitate delivery. Cockers produce long, lean puppies and seldom need delivery by Caesarean section. Put a warm, towel-covered hot-water bottle in a cardboard box and place each newborn puppy inside. Also use this box if you need to transport mother and puppies to the vet's clinic.

SIGNS OF IMMINENT BIRTH

Your bitch will probably refuse food just before she goes into labour. She will restlessly seek out her whelping box and start to tear up the bedding, preparing a nest for her puppies. Her body temperature will drop from her normal 38° C (101° F) to 36° C (97° F), and she may pant. When her waters break and contractions begin, a membrane balloon appears in her vulva and a puppy is imminent. Avoid distractions and keep other animals and strangers away while she is in labour.

Nipples become prominent on large mammary glands

CARE OF THE NEW LITTER

Towel-dry each puppy after it is delivered, clear its nose of mucus, and place it by a teat to suckle. All newborns should squeal and wriggle. During whelping, offer the mother warm milk. Let her rest after labour has ended and all placentas have been delivered. The bitch will need up to four times her normal calorie intake over the next few weeks.

Young puppies suckle greedily

ASSISTING A WEAK OR ABANDONED PUPPY

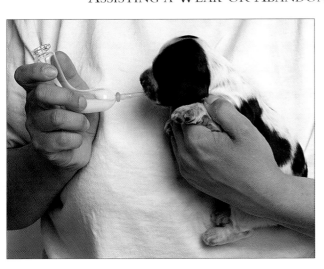

In large, healthy litters where there is not enough milk for all the puppies, or when the mother is incapacitated, use canine milk formula as a supplement. Ask your vet about the correct quantities and bottle feed initially every two to three hours. About one in seven puppies is born small and weak; place a frail puppy near teats offering the best supply of milk. Runts are often the least healthy of the litter, and if left to nature may die within a few days.

GROWING TOGETHER

After about three weeks, the puppies will begin to explore their new environment; by 12 weeks, their senses are fully developed. The most important learning period in a dog's entire life is its first three months, beginning in the mother's nest. If puppies are gently exposed to other animals, people, sights, and sounds during this vital period, they are more likely to develop into well-adjusted, enjoyable adults.

Feed puppies together rather than separately so they will not be possessive over their food as adults

PARTICIPATING IN A SHOW

TAKING PART IN a dog show can be great fun, but both you and your Cocker should be fully prepared. At most shows, Cocker Spaniels are evaluated not only against the other dogs in the show, but also against the judge's interpretation of the ideal physical and personality characteristics for the breed.

MEETING SHOW STANDARDS

Visit a show alone first to see exactly what goes on. While working trials require dogs well trained in obedience or more specialized skills, kennel club events demand only beauty and character. For these, your dog must, at least in your eyes, meet the published Cocker Spaniel or American Cocker breed standard. It should be outgoing, enjoy being handled by strangers, and ideally be a bit of a show-off. No cosmetic aids to improve a dog's appearance are permitted at shows.

PREPARING FOR THE SHOW

As well as transportation needs, make sure that your Cocker is in top physical condition, with clean, tartar-free teeth and wax-free ears. Bathe your dog and trim its nails a few days before the show to allow renewal of the coat's gloss by natural oils. Trim excess feathering from the feet, legs, and chest if necessary.

FAMILY ENJOYMENT

Participating in dog shows requires some hard work, but it should be fun for you, your family, and your dog. At the highest levels of championship showing, breeders take the competitions very seriously and employ professional dog handlers to accompany their dogs in the ring. At all other levels, dog shows are simply a hobby, where the excitement of taking part in an event and building friendships with other Cocker enthusiasts are the real benefits.

ASSESSING MOVEMENT

After the judge has completed a physical examination, your dog's movement is assessed. You will be asked to walk your dog at a trot around the ring; if your dog is hesitant, it will be penalized. The judge also assesses how well you work with your dog – the better the symmetry between you, the higher the score. This is why professional handlers are used in major shows.

COSTS OF SHOWING

Showing your Cocker Spaniel or American Cocker can be inexpensive, or surprisingly costly. If you show your own dog, your only expenses are entry fees, transport, and accommodation. At the highest levels on the show circuit, professional trainers and handlers are often employed. This can be very expensive, and it is a rare dog that is so successful that handling costs are earned back in stud fees or puppy sales. If you are not interested in serious exhibiting, a more sensible approach to showing your Cocker is to consider it a pleasurable but minor pastime for both you and your dog.

THE JUDGE'S INSPECTION

When called into the ring, set your Cocker in its "show stance". Practice at home using food bribes – these are acceptable in the show ring. The judge will examine your dog's body closely, running hands over its skin, feeling the muscles and joints, and inspecting the mouth. Your dog's temperament is being noted all the time – fearful or aggressive dogs never reach the finals of shows.

THE PRIZE-GIVING

After individual assessments, the judge reduces contenders to a shortlist of six or seven dogs. These are examined again, but not as thoroughly as the first time. Finally, the judge awards rosettes for first, second, and third places, and sometimes for "reserve" and "highly commended" as well. Any dog with good health and temperament is just as much a winner as the judges' choices.

SPECIALIZED TRAINING

SOME COCKERS are still bred primarily to work, but this is no longer the case with their American cousins. All Cockers retain their natural flushing and retrieving instincts, however, and many enjoy taking part in hunting, tracking, and obedience or agility trials where they can make use of their natural abilities.

HUNTING, TRACKING, AND FIELD ROLES

WORKING TO THE GUN

Both Cockers and American Cockers retain their instinctive ability to work. American Cockers are rarely seen working not because the skills have been lost, but because of their dense coats. Nevertheless, the skills required to work to the gun must be taught through graduated training with padded retrieves or dead birds. Gentle acclimatization to gunfire is also necessary. On its first successful retrieve of game, there will be as much glee in your Cocker's eyes as there is in yours.

RETRIEVE TRAINING

Retrieving, like all training skills, is grounded in a reliable response to the essential obedience commands "Sit", "Stay", and "Come". (Substitute "Stand" for "Sit" if training for the show ring.) After training your dog to walk to heel, purchase your dog a retrieve dummy and begin retrieve training in a hallway. Unless you are experienced, join the local gundog club.

SELECTING THE RIGHT PUPPY

Virtually all Cockers have excellent noses, soft mouths, and the desire to carry objects. With calm, sensible training, and patience, most puppies can be trained in obedience, agility, scent tracking, or working to the gun. However, some kennels are more successful than others in producing winners in different fields of competition. Field trialling and hunting tests in particular require dogs with speed, instant response to commands, and a highly developed scenting ability. Seek advice from a good trainer on how to select the best puppy for a specific discipline.

ADVANCED OBEDIENCE TRIALS

SUSTAINED LIE-DOWN ON COMMAND

One of the advanced-level obedience trials is a sustained sit or lie-down for as long as 10 minutes with the handler out of sight. Others include close and fast-pace heelwork, retrieves, recalls, distant control, send away-down-return sequences, and scent discrimination.

Competitive obedience training is stimulating for dogs and owners

RETRIEVING A DUMBBELL

As Cockers love to "fetch" and "bring", they have a natural advantage over some breeds in learning to retrieve a dumbbell. Beginning with special small dumbbells, dogs learn to fetch items provided by the trials judges.

TRAINING IN AGILITY

NEGOTIATING OBSTACLES

Cockers are agile and enthusiastic participants in timed agility courses. To enter your Cocker, you must have complete control over your dog, train it to respond well off the lead and tackle obstacles on your command, and be in good physical condition yourself. Like most dogs, Cockers love running through the tunnel.

TIPPING A SEE-SAW

The apparatus used in agility trials includes an "A" frame, hurdles, a tyre, a tunnel, poles to weave through, and a see-saw. Walking the see-saw requires dexterity, confidence, and an instant response to your commands. Enroll your Cocker in a local canine agility club when it is about one year old. Both you and your dog will need patience, but this is excellent activity for Cockers with plenty of mental energy.

BREED STANDARD (COCKER)

A BREED STANDARD is used by the governing kennel club of each country to describe the ideal Cocker Spaniel. Show dogs are judged against this formal index of the unique physical qualities, demeanour, and personality traits that characterize a "perfect" specimen of the breed.

SPANIEL (COCKER)
WORKING GROUP
(Last revised March 1994)

Reproduced by kind permission of
The Kennel Club
London, England

GENERAL APPEARANCE Merry, sturdy, sporting; well balanced; compact; measuring approximately same from withers to ground as from withers to root of tail.

CHARACTERISTICS Merry nature with ever-wagging tail shows a typical bustling movement, particularly when following scent, fearless of heavy cover.

TEMPERAMENT Gentle and affectionate, yet full of life and exuberance.

HEAD AND SKULL Square muzzle, with distinct stop set midway between tip of nose and occiput. Skull well developed, cleanly chiselled, neither too fine nor too coarse. Cheek bones not prominent. Nose sufficiently wide for acute scenting power.

EYES Full, but not prominent. Dark brown or brown, never light, but in the case of liver, liver roan and liver and white, dark hazel to harmonise with coat; with expression of intelligence and gentleness but wide awake, bright and merry; rims tight.

EARS Lobular, set low on a level with eyes. Fine leathers extending to nose tip. Well clothed with long, straight silky hair.

MOUTH Jaws strong with a perfect, regular and complete scissor bite, i.e. upper teeth closely overlapping lower teeth and set square to the jaws.

NECK Moderate in length, muscular. Set neatly into fine sloping shoulders. Clean throat.

FOREQUARTERS Shoulders sloping and fine. Legs well boned, straight, sufficiently short for concentrated power. Not too short to interfere with tremendous exertions expected from this grand, sporting dog.

BODY Strong, compact. Chest well developed and brisket deep; neither too wide nor too narrow in front. Ribs well sprung. Loin short, wide with firm, level topline gently sloping downwards to tail from end of loin to set on of tail.

HINDQUARTERS Wide, well rounded, very muscular. Legs well boned, good bend of stifle, short below hock allowing for plenty of drive.

FEET Firm, thickly padded, cat-like.

TAIL Set on slightly lower than line of back. Must be merry in action and carried level, never cocked up. Customarily docked but never too short to hide, nor too long to interfere with the incessant merry action when working.

GAIT/MOVEMENT True through action with great drive covering ground well.

COAT Flat, silky in texture, never wiry or wavy, not too profuse and never curly. Well feathered forelegs, body and hindlegs above hocks.

COLOUR Various. In self colours no white allowed except on chest.

SIZE Height approximately: dogs: 39–41 cms (15½–16 ins); bitches: 38–39 cms (15–15½ ins). Weight approximately: 12.75–14.5 kgs (28–32 lbs).

FAULTS Any departure from the foregoing points should be considered a fault and the seriousness with which the fault should be regarded should be in exact proportion to its degree.

NOTE Male animals should have two apparently normal testicles fully descended into the scrotum.

GLOSSARY

BRISKET The forepart of the body below the chest between forelegs.

DOCK To shorten tail by cutting.

FEATHERING Longer fringe of hair on ears, legs, tail or body.

FOREARM The bone of the forelegs between elbow and wrist.

FORELEG The front leg from elbow to foot.

FOREQUARTERS Front part of dog excluding head and neck.

GAIT The pattern of footsteps at various rates of speed, each pattern distinguished by a particular rhythm and footfall.

GUNDOG A dog trained to work to find live game and/or retrieve game that has been shot or wounded.

HIND LEG Leg from pelvis to foot.

HINDQUARTERS Rear part of dog from loin.

HOCK The tarsus or collection of bones of the hind leg forming the joint between the second thigh and the metatarsus.

LIVER A colour, also known as brown or chocolate.

LOIN Region of body either side of vertebral column between last ribs and the hindquarters.

MUZZLE The head in front of the eyes, nasal bone, nostrils, and jaws; foreface.

OCCIPUT Upper, back point of skull.

ROAN A fine mixture of coloured hairs alternating with white hairs; blue roan, orange roan, lemon roan, liver roan, etc.

SELF COLOUR One colour or whole colour except for lighter shadings.

SKULL Bony regions of head. Usually meant as section of head from stop to occiput.

SLOPING SHOULDERS The shoulder blade set obliquely or "laid back".

SOFT MOUTH Gentle grip on a retrieve.

STIFLE The joint of the hind leg between the thigh and the second thigh; the dog's knee.

STOP The step up from muzzle to skull; indentation between the eyes where the nasal bone and skull meet.

TOPLINE The dog's outline from just behind the withers to the tail set.

WELL SPRUNG RIBS Ribs springing out from spinal column giving correct shape.

WITHERS The highest point of the body, immediately behind the neck.

BREED STANDARD (AMERICAN)

A BREED STANDARD is a description of the American Cocker Spaniel as decided by the governing kennel club of each country. It is a formal index against which show dogs are judged and includes the physical qualities, demeanour, and personality traits that typify a "perfect" breed specimen.

SPANIEL (AMERICAN COCKER)
WORKING GROUP
(Last revised March 1994)

Reproduced by kind permission of
The Kennel Club
London, England

GENERAL APPEARANCE Serviceable-looking dog with refined chiselled head, strong, well boned legs, well up at the shoulder, compact sturdy body, wide muscular quarters, well balanced.

CHARACTERISTICS Merry, free, sound, keen to work.

TEMPERAMENT Equable with no suggestion of timidity.

HEAD AND SKULL Well developed and rounded, neither flat nor domed. Eyebrows and stop clearly defined. Median line distinctly marked to rather more than half-way up crown. Area surrounding eye socket well chiselled. Distance from tip of nose to stop approximately one-half distance from stop up over crown to base of skull. Muzzle broad, deep, square, even jaws. Nose well developed. Nostrils black in black and tans, black or brown in buffs, browns, brown and tans, roans and parti-colours.

EYES Eyeballs round, full and looking directly forward. Shape of eyerims gives a slightly almond appearance. Neither weak nor goggled. Expression intelligent, alert, soft and appealing. Colour of iris dark brown to black in blacks, black and tans, buffs and creams, and in the darker shades of parti-colours and roans. In reds

and browns, dark hazel; in parti-colours and roans of lighter shades, not lighter than hazel; the darker the better.

EARS Lobular, set on line no higher than lower part of eyes, leather fine and extending to nostrils, well clothed with long silky, straight or wavy hair.

MOUTH Jaws strong with a perfect, regular and complete scissor bite, i.e. upper teeth closely overlapping lower teeth and set square to the jaws.

NECK Long, muscular and free from throatiness. Rising strongly and slightly arched.

FOREQUARTERS Shoulders deep, clean-cut and sloping without protrusion, so set that upper points of withers at an angle permitting wide spring of ribs. Forelegs straight, strongly boned and muscular, set close to body well under scapulae. Elbows well let down, turning neither in nor out. Pasterns short and strong.

BODY Height at withers approximating length from withers to set on of tail. Chest deep. Lowest point no higher than elbows, front sufficiently wide for adequate heart and lung space, yet not so wide as to interfere with straight forward movement of forelegs. Ribs deep and well sprung throughout. Body short in couplings and flank, with depth at flank somewhat less than at last rib. Back strong, sloping evenly and slightly downwards from withers to set of tail. Hips wide with quarters well rounded and muscular. Body appearing short, compact and firmly knit together, giving impression of strength. Never appearing long and low.

HINDQUARTERS Strongly boned, muscled with good angulation at stifle and powerful, clearly defined thighs. Stifle joint strong without slippage. Hocks strong, well let down; when viewed from behind, hindlegs parallel when in motion or at rest.

FEET Compact, not spreading, round and firm, with deep, strong, tough pads and hair between toes; facing truly forward.

TAIL Customarily docked by three-fifths of tail. Set on and carried on a line with top line of back or slightly higher, never straight up and never so low as to indicate timidity. When dog in motion merry tail action.

GAIT/MOVEMENT Co-ordinated, smooth and effortless, covering ground well.

COAT On head, short and fine; on body, medium length, with enough under coating to give protection. Ears, chest, abdomen and legs well feathered, but not so excessive as to hide body lines or impede movement and function as a sporting dog. Texture most important. Coat silky, flat or slightly wavy. Excessive coat, curly, woolly or cotton texture undesirable.

COLOUR
BLACKS: Jet black; shadings of brown or liver in sheen of coat undesirable. Black and tan and brown and tan (classified under solid colours) having definite tan markings on jet black or brown body. Tan markings distinct and plainly visible and colour of tan may be from lightest cream to darkest red colour. Amount of tan markings restricted to ten per cent or less of colour of specimen; tan markings in excess of ten per cent undesirable. Tan markings not readily visible in ring or absence of tan markings

in any of specified locations undesirable. Tan markings located as follows:

1 A clear spot over each eye.
2 On sides of muzzle and on cheeks.
3 On underside of ears.
4 On all feet and legs.
5 Under tail.
6 On chest, optional, presence or absence permissible.

Tan on muzzle which extends upwards and joins over muzzle highly undesirable. Any solid colour other than black of uniform shades. Lighter colouring of feathering permissible. In all above solid colours a small amount of white on chest and throat while not desirable, permissible, but white in any other location highly undesirable.

PARTI-COLOURS: Two or more definite colours appearing in clearly defined markings essential. Primary colour which is ninety per cent or more highly undesirable; secondary colour or colours which are limited solely to one location also highly undesirable. Roans are classified as parti-colours and may be of any usual roaning patterns. Tricolours, any of above colours combined with tan markings. Tan markings preferably located in same pattern as for black and tan.

SIZE Ideal height: (the word approximate leaves too much to chance.) dogs: 36.25–38.75 cms (14½–15½ ins); bitches: 33.75–36.25 cms (13½–14½ ins).

FAULTS Any departure from the foregoing points should be considered a fault and the seriousness with which the fault should be regarded should be in exact proportion to its degree.

NOTE Male animals should have two apparently normal testicles fully descended into the scrotum.

INDEX

ACKNOWLEDGMENTS

AUTHOR'S ACKNOWLEDGMENTS

Many thanks to Phil Hunt, Sarah Lillicrapp, Wendy Bartlet, Helen Thompson, and their efficient DK production team, and to Patricia Holden White for choreographing several photographic sessions. Further thanks to Dr. Gary Clayton Jones for X-rays of joint disease, Dr. Sheila Crispin at the University of Bristol's Department of Clinical and Veterinary Science for information on and photos of Cocker Spaniel inherited eye problems, to Dr. Peter Kertesz for data on teeth, and Dr. Ivan Burger at the Waltham Centre for Pet Nutrition for detailed advice on the Cocker Spaniel's energy requirements. Finally, my thanks to the veterinarians worldwide who helped with information on Cocker Spaniel behaviour.

PUBLISHER'S ACKNOWLEDGMENTS

Dorling Kindersley would like to thank photographer Tracy Morgan for her invaluable contribution to the book. Also special thanks to Tracy's photographic assistants: K. Cuthbert, Sally Bergh-Roose, and Stella Smyth-Carpenter. We are also very grateful to Patricia Holden White for her generous advice and help on photographic sessions. Thanks also to Karin Woodruff for the index. Finally, we would like to thank the following people for lending their dogs and/or for modelling:

Wendy Bartlet; Andy Bone and Chris Dewar-Dixon and "Missy"; Stephanie Carpenter; Sue Cox; Natalie Cummings and Nickendebby Surprise; Kuryan M. Cuthbert; Anne Daniels and "Topaz" (Starbourne Tiger Lily); Mr. and Mrs. Fishlocks and "Toby"; Cheryl Frith and "Toby" (Trantripps Fossy Bear) and "Louis" (Trantripps Fortunate Sun); Chris and Tanya Goddard and "Rufus" (Nataya Chucklebot); Hilary Hill and Princehill Joy at Christmas; Paula Hull (member of the British Grooming Team) and "Colin" (Ashenberry Rocket Socks), "Emily" (Ashenberry Love Boots), "Jaffa" (Ashenberry Orange Delight), and the puppies of Ashenberry Bless My Boots and Ashenberry Moon Boots; Phil Hunt; Sue and Annie Kettle and Lujesa Happy Too, Lujesa Summer Breeze, and Sh. Champion Lujesa Fiorucci; Sarah Lillicrapp; Jennifer Lloyd-Carey and Falconers Reprint of Ware; Gemma Marcham; Daniel McCarthy; Tracy Morgan and "Scorch" (Topkyri The Fire Dragon), "Spicy" (Craigleith The Painted Lady), "Flame" (Topkyri The Fire Dancer), "Topper" (Craigleith Music Man), and "Kyri" (Craigleith Waltz Of The Flowers); Mr. and Mrs. Richardson and Fionnrua Frangelica and Cardamine Choc Tannin; Mrs. Mollie Robinson and Craigleith Merry Widow Waltz; Hesta Small; Clare Stamp; Helen Thompson; Mr. and Mrs. Walker and Cardamine Cardinal, Cardamine Georgia Brown, Cardamine Choc Tannin, and Cardamine Coffee Chocolates; Lyn Ward and "Ned" (Merrielms Cockney Rebel) and "Polly" (Emsdale Blue Mist at Merrielms); and Evelyn and Hilary White and Am. Champion J.P.K. Simply Snazzy at Tantripp, "Lucy" (Tantripp Could It Be Magic), Tantripp Brown Velvet, and "Annie" (Tantripp Hot Fudge Sundae).

PHOTOGRAPHIC CREDITS

Every effort has been made to trace the copyright holders, and we apologize in advance for any unintentional omissions. We would be pleased to insert the appropriate acknowledgments in any subsequent edition of this publication.

Key: l=left, r=right, t=top, c=centre, a=above, b=below

All photography by Tracy Morgan except:
Animal Photography: (Sally Anne Thompson) 8tl; **Ardea:** 62cl; **Christopher Bradbury:** 66cr; **Bridgeman Art Library, London:** (Bonhams, London) 64cl; (British Library, London) 6cr; (Giraudon) 62cr; **Dr. Sheila Crispin:** 54; **John Darling:** 6bl, 72br; **Jack Davey:** 9tr; **Dr. Peter Kertesz:** 46br; **Dave King:** 1, 16tl, 16br, 17br, 18br, 20br, 21bl, 55, 70tl; **Tim Ridley:** 17tr, 41cr, 42–43, 66br, 68–69; **Science Photo Library:** (Jackie Lewin) 52bl; (David Scharf) 52cl; **The Image Bank:** (Lynn M. Stone) 6tl; **David Ward:** 22cl, 57br; **Wood Green Animal Shelters:** 22tr; **Zefa:** 2.

ILLUSTRATIONS

Samantha Elmhurst: 53, 55, 67;
Angelika Elsebach: 58–59;
Jane Pickering: 37;
Clive Spong: 11, 13.